ALMOST ALCHEMY

ALMOST ALCHEMY

HOW TO USE **DYNAMIC**
FINANCIAL EFFICIENCIES & STRATEGIES

to make any business of any size produce
MORE FROM FEWER AND LESS

BY DAN S. KENNEDY

INCLUDES:
THE FOUND MONEY MAP®

and special guest expert chapter by
TIMOTHY SEWARD
CEO, ROI REVOLUTION

ForbesBooks

ABOUT THIS BOOK

Dan Kennedy has been our secret. He has been influencing our business for the better, in various ways, for more than 20 years. We have depended on him. In this book, he lays out a case for efficiency and practicality in business thinking that will leave you humbled and excited at the same time. It's a can't-put-down, must-read map for business success leveraging the principles of direct marketing that Dan Kennedy has taught so well for so long.

GREG RENKER

Co-Founder, Guthy-Renker Corporation

The company's created, billion dollar brands include Proactiv® and Crepe Erase®.

• • •

I shudder to think what my competition could do with the insights and information in this book, but I also know that the businesses' leaders who need these strategies the most are the least likely to read them. Another eye-opening work by Dan Kennedy, that rarest of breeds: a master of his craft, actively applying the most powerful direct-response marketing strategies, but also able to teach them, not as theory but in straight-forward and actionable ways.

DR. DUSTIN BURLESON, DDS, MBA

BurlesonSeminars.com

Dr. Burleson developed five successful orthodontic practices, an in-profession publishing company, and training, consulting and coaching for over 1,000 practices

• • •

For two decades, Dan Kennedy has been the somewhat secret weapon in my businesses. His genius and guidance has helped me go from 6-figures in debt to a multi-million dollar global business. I've also been privileged to witness the impact of his strategies deployed in thousands of others' entrepreneurial ventures, of every imaginable type and size. These transformations look to outside observers *like magic.*

But there is a concealed structure to all magic, and in this book – Almost Alchemy – Dan Kennedy has revealed that structure.

CHRIS CARDELL

CardellMedia.com

Chris is the U.K. and Europe's leading authority on online marketing, including successful, profitable uses of Google, Facebook and other social media. His company re-makes and then manages web sites, online marketing systems, and online ad spend and traffic generation for hundreds of small to mid-sized business. Chris also acts as a business consultant and personal coach to entrepreneurs.

• • •

Having worked with thousands of business owners who exit and sell their companies after investing a life's work in them, I can state one true dictum: the businesses with the most profit sell for the highest prices. Everything Dan Kennedy has said in this book about profit is accurate, insightful and valuable. Most businesses are weak in financial efficiencies. This book can change that.

TED OAKLEY

OxbowAdvisers.com

Ted is the author of a number of books for business owners including $20-MILLION AND BROKE, is frequently seen on Fox Business, on the Stuart Varney and Neil Cavuto programs, and has a robust video and print media platform at his own firm's web site.

• • •

When people ask me how I went from a dead-broke high school drop-out to the CEO of a thriving, profitable multi-million dollar business, debt free, in the top 1% of income earners, I give them one name: *Dan Kennedy*.

I read and study everything he produces, and by his written work, recorded material, and as a trusted source of advice, he has been one of the most influential, pivotal people in my life. THIS BOOK is nothing short of brilliant and should be thought of as required reading for any entrepreneur or CEO.

ROBIN ROBINS

CEO, Technology Marketing Toolkit Inc., TechnologyMarketingToolkit.com

Robin has built the largest and most successful 'consultant to the consultants' business in the technology field, with top-tier corporate partners and sponsors, an international legion of consultants relying on her training, coaching and support, and along with it all, an amazing reputation well beyond the borders of her niche.

. . .

ALMOST ALCHEMY is a unique take on real world direct marketing, re-thought, brilliantly clarified, with applications for ANY business. Only Dan Kennedy could write this book – *or would.* In a world full of imposters and charlatans, I make it standard operating procedure to seek out Dan for his latest thinking. This *instant classic* begins like a parable, continues as an instruction manual, and ends as a business reference to be referred to regularly – particularly his Found Money Map. This is only "almost" alchemy if you fail to apply it. Any one of this book's insights could trigger breakthroughs in a business. One gem here was the secret to our $50-Million book operation at Boardroom. Get into this book and mine it.

BRIAN KURTZ

CEO, Titans of Direct Marketing

Author, *The Advertising Solution and Overdeliver*

Brian worked alongside the legendary Marty Edelston in building Boardroom Inc. from 'kitchen table' to one of the largest direct-to-consumer book and newsletter publishers in the world, best-known for its BottomLine newsletters. Since exiting Boardroom, he has been a highly valued and effective advisor to entrepreneurs and executives, and his Titans of Direct Marketing mastermind groups have fast become THE place to be, to create transformative business ideas and mega-growth.

ABOUT DAN KENNEDY'S ENTIRE BODY OF WORK

I have always admired Dan Kennedy's ability to see the vital truths in *any* business and to state these realities with straight language and clear definitions. His approach is direct. His ideas are controversial. His ability to get results for his clients is unchallenged,

BRIAN TRACY

BrianTracy.com

Brian Tracy is a prolific author and one of this era's leading professional speakers, a globe-trotter, a deep thinker, and a life's work devoted to decoding business and personal success.

• • •

Dan Kennedy's smart, direct, forceful advice has been of great value to our business. I wish I'd had it back when we started Joan Rivers Products. It would have made that journey much easier. Every time I see him, I tell him he's a genius, and I don't compliment lightly.

JOAN RIVERS

The late Joan Rivers was not only one of the most brilliant entertainers of her time, but also an extraordinary entrepreneur. Dan Kennedy worked with her on several projects and they became personal friends.

• • •

....there are even parts of your *business* writing that are as good as Tom Wolfe's! And I should know. I published an original 7,500 word piece by Mr. Wolfe.

RICH KARLGAARD

Editor, *Forbes Magazine*

Published by ForbesBooks, Charleston, South Carolina.
Member of Advantage Media Group.

ForbesBooks is a registered trademark, and the ForbesBooks colophon is a trademark of Forbes Media, LLC.

Printed in the United States of America.

10 9 8 7 6 5 4 3 2 1

ISBN: 978-1-950863-23-5
LCCN: 2019915296

Cover design by George Stevens.
Layout design by Matthew Morse.

This publication is designed to provide accurate and authoritative information in regard to the subject matter covered. It is sold with the understanding that the publisher is not engaged in rendering legal, accounting, or other professional services. If legal advice or other expert assistance is required, the services of a competent professional person should be sought.

Advantage Media Group is proud to be a part of the Tree Neutral® program. Tree Neutral offsets the number of trees consumed in the production and printing of this book by taking proactive steps such as planting trees in direct proportion to the number of trees used to print books. To learn more about Tree Neutral, please visit **www.treeneutral.com**.

Since 1917, the Forbes mission has remained constant. Global Champions of Entrepreneurial Capitalism. ForbesBooks exists to further that aim by bringing the Stories, Passion, and Knowledge of top thought leaders to the forefront. ForbesBooks brings you The Best in Business. To be considered for publication, please visit **www.forbesbooks.com**.

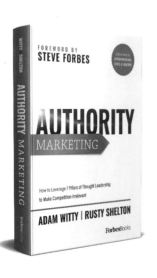

THIS IS A PIECE OF A DOLLAR BILL.

It represents business at its core. A business is *a device* from which dollar bills exit and into which dollar bills arrive. The idea is that fewer will leave than arrive, thereby accumulating assets inside the business and permitting transfer of some of retained dollar bills to the business' owners and shareholders. Whether this happy result occurs or not, and if so, to what extent is largely determined by how *efficient* the business' operators are with the dollars entering and exiting.

Ideally, many or most of the dollars departing act as *homing pigeon dollars*. They leave briefly only to return fatter than when they left. The dollar returns as $1.30, $1.80, $2.20, or $22.00. It is then divided back up into dollars, each a new homing pigeon dollar, each released out the window into the wild, each returning fatter than when it left. And again. And again. This is called *Direct-Response Advertising** and

Direct Marketing*. This is where I *live*.

(*NOT to be confused with ordinary Advertising, which is a very, very lazy and unreliable pigeon. NOT to be confused with ordinary Marketing, also a lazy and unreliable and costly to feed pigeon.)

A dollar bill can, sadly, be reduced to a piece of itself before exiting to go to work. A weakened, wounded homing pigeon dollar. By various kinds of ignorance, stupidity and malfeasance, a dollar scheduled to leave on a mission can be reduced to .70, .60, .40 before getting a chance to get out there and get to work. This tragedy *is* going on in *your* business right now. You'll know where to look for it by this book.

A dollar bill can, happily, become $1.10, $1.30, $2.00 "magically" <u>before</u> exiting to go to work. A stronger, mightier, more effective homing pigeon dollar. By various kinds of know-how, creativity and cleverness, a dollar scheduled to leave on a mission can be increased by .40, .60, .70 before getting out there and getting to work. This exciting alchemy *can* go on in *your* business. You'll know how, by this book.

TABLE OF CONTENTS

FOREWORD

(not to be skipped)

CHANGE YOUR MATH
CHANGE YOUR BUSINESS
CHANGE YOUR LIFE

The sustainability of a business and the wealth to be extracted from a company by its owners are **not** products of brand identity or strength, product category leadership, superiority of goods or services, gross revenues or even net profits. *None* of these things guarantee sustainability or guarantee wealth extraction.

I am going to tell you what <u>does</u> insure sustainability and wealth extraction, but first a few words about how many things *don't*, that business owners are led to focus on and sometimes bullied into obsessing over. That list is long and mushrooming. There is a literal conspiracy of charlatans, con artists, promoters and dunces **acting in concert *to get you to count the wrong things***.

This has multiplied with online, so-called e-commerce, and social media, for which you are told to count "new metrics"; likes, views, viral re-tweets, and just about anything else *but* money. But this only the newest incarnation of a time-honored deception. Advertisers have long been told to count eyes and ears; readers, viewers and listeners. With print, a mysterious pass-along readership for which no accurate count is remotely possible. Distraction from factual accountability has long been the actual stock 'n trade of purveyors of media and the agencies and experts that encircle it.

In the months I was finishing this, revelations of this nature were exposed involving Facebook, Google, YouTube and Twitter. Fake accounts, fake fans and followers, fake views, and more. Some of it by their just turning a blind eye; some by their own hands. Either way, advertisers scammed. In one 48 hour purge of fake accounts at Twitter (July 2018), Katy Perry had 2.8-million fake fans disappear overnight, a body count by which compensation to her from sponsors, and general power in the marketplace was based. Big corporate advertisers quietly got and get rebates from media and agencies when the fraud is caught. But most rank-n-file advertisers (like you) never know you're being taken advantage of. Having your pockets picked. You are just left to wonder why *your* results are so inexplicably disappointing.

Gypsies, Tramps & Thieves

Within my very first year in the advertising business, I realized We – the entire gaggle of media, agencies and related "professionals" – were engaged in a grand deception, if not an outright criminal enterprise, at the expense of deliberately confused clients. I didn't want to be a part of it, so I departed to *direct*-response advertising and *direct* marketing, where there is at least *some* honor among thieves. Some factual, financial, ROI accountability.

Over 46 years in dispensing strategic advertising, marketing, business and financial advice at all levels --- small business to Fortune 500 --- I have witnessed an on-going, deliberate obfuscation about return on investment realities by pretty much everybody profiteering by providing advertising and marketing and media to clients.

This book is my attempt at truth and clarity in place of obfuscation and confusion.

You are to be *somewhat* forgiven for falling victim to the smoke machines and their operators.

When it seems *everybody* is doing "x," and *everybody* is telling you to judge the value of doing that "x" in a certain way, and those you look to or are referred to or see celebrated for their wisdom verifies what you see and are told about "x," it is damnably hard to be the conscientious objector, the skeptic, the outlier. Yet there is an important saying, Russian I think: only dead fish swim _with_ the stream. I know *exactly* how hard it is to be swimming in the opposite direction of all the other fish and against the prevailing, popular currents because I've been doing it my entire career. The difficulty of it does not, however, excuse you from the responsibility to do it, especially when facts favoring the road less traveled present themselves to you.

So, what is THE most important guarantor of business sustainability and wealth extraction, if it is not any of the above mentioned things?

It is: financial efficiency.

That means getting the absolute maximum possible value out of each and every dollar invested, preferably quickly and repetitively. *That* is *the* thing to find ways to accurately measure and count. *That* is the thing to work on improving, on kaizen-ing, most assiduously, most aggressively.

A company has to be purposefully engineered (or re-engineered) for financial efficiency, and the adherence to that engineering schematic relentlessly enforced. If you have bad money-math and you replace it with good money-math you will dramatically change everything else for the better. **Any and every way you find by this book to CHANGE YOUR MATH FOR THE BETTER, every other thing will follow right along wagging its tail, for the better.**

As a personal side note, I was once quite poor, broke, bankrupt. In struggle, I tried changing many things. But none of it mattered until I learned to change my math. Then everything else changed. There is a saying I first heard from Joan Rivers, a friend: when you have enough $100 bills in your pocket, you are handsome and you sing well too. It's not *that* simple. Maybe not *that* crass. But I know from intimate personal experience just how powerful changes in one's money-math can be in and of themselves and in leading and enabling other changes, by you, and in the way the world sees and responds to you. This is true on a personal, individual level and it is just as true in business and business environments.

As you come to a broad and deep familiarity with financial efficiency and the means of achieving maximum financial efficiency by this book, you will realize it is the last thing anybody in or vending to or otherwise involved with your business is talking to you about or encouraging you to think about. It should dominate everyone's concerns and begin and end every conversation. Instead, it is relegated to the furthest, dimmest lit corner of your enterprise, chained to the wall, and gagged.

I am the only person who is going to urge you to un-chain it and give it the most important seat next to yours, and make it your co-pilot.

You are most fortunate to have found me! ☺

I am mostly known as an Ad Man, not a finance guy. Most clients come to me for advertising, marketing and selling strategies, and are initially surprised that I refuse to separate these from a business' financial efficiency. I can claim no academic or similar credential for this – only 40+ years under the hoods of thousands of businesses, intimately working with people building small, medium and large companies in diverse fields, making millionaires and multi-millionaires. And a reputation for "NO B.S.," which became a brand. I know from nearly universal experience that you probably do <u>NOT</u> need a better ad campaign, more ad or marketing media used, a brand or message re-boot, or any of the similar things that bring clients to my door. At least, not now; not yet; not disconnected from the context of financial efficiency. Almost every client comes to get external things done but hardly any escape my insistent re-engineering of their internal business.

Financial Engineering or Re-Engineering is the art, science and process of adding, subtracting and rearranging everything in order to achieve maximum possible financial efficiency.

If for no other reason, this is vital so that you can greatly outspend all competitors in investments in new customer acquisition and in customer retention. This is the secret of growth, of power: being able to spend A LOT MORE on getting and keeping each customer than anyone else in your category can or will. Without, of course, going bankrupt. Financially inefficient companies can never dream of such a strategy. They are boxed in, imprisoned, and made weak by having to do the opposite: spend as little as possible, only using the "cheapest" means of acquiring customers. They are 4' 5", 98-pound weaklings trying to play pro football. You really do not want to be that deficient little guy lined up across from a 6' 3", 340-pound, drooling, grunting, nails-for-breakfast Neanderthal, with out of the blocks speed of a gazelle and mindset of an assassin.

In this book, we will look at more than 20 different categories of empowering Financial Engineering and Financial Efficiency. We'll also later return to the premise just stated, probably THE most important piece of strategic advice, and the hardest to digest piece of advice in the entire book.

It's highly doubtful they'll all apply to your business. Many can. Any one can effect a significant difference in the business' sustainability and in your extraction of wealth from it.

To the latter, one philosophical item: wealth extraction by you, for you, is THE point of starting, buying, building, owning a business. If you are familiar with Ayn Rand, you can characterize this as Ayn Rand-ian, on the most pragmatic level. Business owners are constantly beaten about head and shoulders with rolled up newspapers, to persuade them to place others' needs and priorities and 'obligations' to customers, employees, communities above their own. Do *not* mistake this for some moral case being made by saints and angels, better souls than you. It is nothing more or less than craven manipulation for their own selfish purposes, be that political power or applying balm to their envy and resentment (better treated by honest ambition, initiative, investment and persistence). They are, in their own ways, just as Ayn Rand-ian as I am or you might ever be. They just wear disguises. I do not. I am here to tell you that you should *never* feel apologetic or unreasonably harsh for demanding maximum financial efficiency, for engaging in whatever financial engineering is necessary to get it, and for extracting wealth from your business by doing so.

Know that all resistance is, at best, uninformed, but more likely either fear-based, in perceiving threats to their self-interest, or resentment based, in reaction to wounds to ego. Much of what I lay out in this book will brook resistance. That's not a fault, but rather a sign of its truth and validity and importance. The more who find this objectionable, and the more objectionable they find it, the more confidence you should have in it. Fact is, the majority in general or the majority of any industry, profession or otherwise gathered group is always wrong – especially about money and success.

Walt Disney said his only Bad Days At The Office were those rare occasions when everybody thought his latest idea was a good one. On those days, he went home depressed. This principle is even truer applied to a philosophy of rational self-interest and earned privilege and prosperity. Most people around you won't approve. That's good. If they did, it'd be a lousy idea and we'd have to go home depressed.

We are embarking here on a path with only one purpose: you, the owner, operator, chief cook 'n bottle washer, person at risk, captain left out of the life boats, to go down with the ship should it sink getting as rich as possible from your business. If it's a bigger enterprise, then you and your invested shareholders stand side by side. But everyone else and every other consideration take seats at the back of your bus. *Your* bus.

CHAPTER 1

A Romantic and Respectful
RELATIONSHIP WITH MONEY

"Making money is Art. Working is Art. And good business is the best Art."

- Andy Warhol

MONEY IS **MOBILE.**
MONEY IS **RATIONAL.**
MONEY IS **AGNOSTIC.**

I risk losing you, by opening with this subject, but it is foundational for everything else in this book. Later you'll find *very* pragmatic, practical things to do, and most will be happier with those chapters than with this one. This is more about: how to think, in order to be empowered as an alchemist. It is admittedly a relatively esoteric dissertation. Please give me, and it, a chance!

Money operates entirely on its own self-interest, so it goes where it is welcomed, respected and appreciated, and it is mobile, and an escape artist, so it cannot be long held captive in a hostile environment or kept where it is taken for granted.

This is why money flows out of New Jersey to Florida and from California to Texas. This is why a company loses customers or loses favor with shareholders: money has packed up and is moving on.

Admittedly this is a metaphysical approach to wealth and a personification of money that many find appropriate only for the weekend weirdo retreat in Sedona, not the corporate boardroom – but they are wrong. Forced to describe Munger in one word, Buffett chose "rational." But even hard-nosed Charlie Munger says "You can't ignore the fact that money has its own decision-making."

The Money Secret Rich Individuals & "Genius" CEOs Know, That They Are Scared To Talk About For Fear Of Being Laughed Out Of The Room

There *is* an 'energy of money.'

Alignment with it, syncing with it is possible and powerful. Acting in conflict with it is dangerous and destructive.

I have spent my entire life around made-from-scratch millionaire and multi-millionaire entrepreneurs who raise themselves up in large part because they develop a different understanding of and relationship with money than everybody else's, the masses', even the academic and corporate executive mentalities. I can tell you, privately if not publicly, they think of money in a humanized way, and believe *it* has a rational mind of *its* own and nearly omnipotent powers to act on *its* thoughts. If you let yourself engage in a relationship with it like this, you can begin to weigh a very simple equation: *if I were money, and this was said or done to me, would I stay or go elsewhere? Be attracted or angry, resentful, repelled?*

How do you feel about having to sleep in a dirty hotel room? Well, how does money think about having to hang out in a restaurant's dirty kitchen, unclean or badly worn booths, smelly bathrooms?

Money is always in motion. The amount of money in motion is quite mind-boggling. Anybody who claims a shortage is myopic. When someone says their business is suffering because of a bad economy, they are actually talking about *their* economy. With the exception of relatively temporary, truly cataclysmic economic events like the Great Depression of 1929, there is actually no such thing as '*the* economy.' Instead, there are aspects of it that are "bad" while at the same time aspects that are "good." This is simply the money moving or moved from one place and one group of people to another. If you acknowledge and respect its mobility, you will constantly be thinking about where it is likely to migrate to next, then placing yourself there just ahead of it or at least moving right along with it.

Conrad Hilton bought up hotels during the Great Depression, confident that a boom had to follow, and that it would put more business travelers on the road than ever before – all needing lodging and meeting rooms. He saw where money would be arriving and acted accordingly. He did not, incidentally, have a mountain of research assembled by MBAs and consultancies to base his future vision on. Had he waited for that, he'd have been too late.

Money moves about geographically. The U.S. has 50 states, but as I write this only 7 growth states. California, once upon a time the place money was migrating to from every other nook 'n cranny of the country is now but 3 steps away from mass exodus.

It moves about demographically. Age, affluence, politics, all predict spending. I've written about this extensively, specific to marketing, in several books in my NO B.S. series, including *No BS Guide to Marketing to the Affluent, 3rd Edition* and *No BS Guide to Marketing to Boomers and Seniors.* Marijuana dispensaries located in or adjacent to upscale, high-end retirement communities are certain to generate greater profits per square foot than those next to college campuses. Iger wisely bought Marvel for Disney, to stem the losses of its customers when they reached teen age.

It moves by invention, innovation, replacement of products, services, media, although this is exaggerated in importance in most business leaders' minds. And, it can exit by this stimulus, as much as it can arrive. The entire home security industry, featuring multi-thousand dollar system sales and installations and highly profitable "monitoring" is watching all the money exit, moving quickly to commoditized, cheap, simple consumer products like the Ring® video doorbell or SimpliSafe® alarms.

'Place Strategy' As A Prime Opportunity To Move With Money And To Profit By Moving Money

Sam Walton made Wal-Mart by recognizing there was a lot of money hanging out in small towns and rural America, being ignored and disrespected by the retail industry. Magic Johnson made fortunes with movie theaters and licensed Starbucks stores planted in urban inner cities with almost entirely black populations, because he recognized there was a surprising amount of money there, being ignored and disrespected. He ultimately opened 125 Starbucks stores in these markets, then sold the entire thing back to Starbucks, for a fortune. Both performed alchemy by Place Strategy. Media is Place, too. My long-time client Guthy-Renker built a billion dollar company with

TV infomercials, recognizing that there was a lot of money moving around from midnight to 6 A.M. and on weekends, in the hands of people with their TVs on, remote controls in hand, looking for *something* to watch. This was money being largely ignored by traditional advertisers.

As an investor, I was initially very skeptical of and disinterested in Amazon. The business of online bookselling, then online retailing seemed highly questionable to me. But when I came to understand that people were going to use online search to shop for products and services, I saw Amazon as a search engine *used by buyers*. I bought most of the Amazon stock I own at about $14.00 a share. Money was moving to Amazon for the same reason that made the original search engine for shoppers – the Yellow Pages – thrive. The old Yellow Pages slogan "Let your fingers do the walking" is even more accurate in describing Amazon. In that light, it was clear to me, money was moving from an old house to a new house in the same city, leaving one neighborhood blighted while turning another neighborhood into the new beehive of activity, the new place of prosperity.

Money no longer wanted to turn pages, read ads, and make phone calls. It wanted to just click.

By the way, my friend Ken McCarthy was credited by no less than *Time Magazine* in its heyday as the first person to understand and commercialize pay-per-click. Ken was way ahead of his time in recognizing and developing the commercial possibilities of the internet. He first spoke publicly on the subject at a conference of mine in 1993. *1993.* Go back and check out 1993. Neither Bill Gates nor Steve Jobs had any interest or belief in the internet as the next new marketplace. In essence, Ken saw where money was moving – and why – before most others did. This is, of course, *the* question.

Predicting the near and long term future movements of money and being there ahead of it or with it is how you keep a mature business alive, how you leapfrog a fledgling business over its competition.

Prescience is extremely valuable, but does not require mystical clairvoyant powers. It can be founded on a deep understanding of money's motivations and movements.

I make and publish a lot of business, financial, societal and trend predictions in my speeches and newsletters and books, and I have an impressive track record of being proved right 3, 5, 7 years after my first remarks on a subject. More often than not, these predictions are based on my thinking about money's likely thinking about the matter. Deep Throat famously told Woodward and Bernstein: "Follow the money," as his clue to Watergate. In business, following it can be a tad late, although doing so is far superior to stubbornly ignoring its movements. But it is better to *anticipate* its movement.

Ask Money: *What Do YOU Think About This?*

When I hear a "news item" of almost any sort, I automatically ask myself if money will have an opinion about it? React to it? Move because of it? For entrepreneurs, I write about this in *The No B.S. Marketing Letter* (www.nobsinnercircle.com).

So, here is the hardest-to-swallow, most difficult decision to make from this book: whether or not to consciously and deliberately craft a personal, romantic, respectful relationship with money – or to dismiss this as hooey. Whether to talk about money's motivations and relationship with money by your business openly with associates (risking being judged crazy) – or to keep this your secret (greatly reducing its power).

This can be a creative way of breaking the link between what you sell and what you do in the marketplace. All existing businesses are hampered by this link. _The_ start point of all the common thinking is: who can we sell this to? How? What will make them want it? How can we sell more of it? How can we protect its pricing? This forecloses all other start-points, notably including how are the market's interests and requirements changing? You can widen your view and broaden your thought by _not_ thinking about your existing products (or services; distribution channels; sales methods, etc.) at all and instead asking questions about where money has moved from, what it has stopped supporting, and by those same motivations, where it might go and what might it support next? – in your general category of commerce, but not narrowed to your business' specifics.

A caution must be issued. Be careful you are accurately assessing, following and by facts attempting to predict the movement of _money._ It does not necessarily, _proportionately_ move with popular activity or "traffic." For example, traffic has moved from brick-and-mortar to online places and from offline to online media in much, much greater quantity than has money. The facts about the percentage of commerce occurring online are very, very, very different from the mythology. However, money is moving away from facilitating human interactions and socializing to isolation and relationships with machines; with A.I., and that can't be ignored. The place where this trend is furthest advanced is Japan, where sex arranged by humans with humans is increasingly judged just too much trouble, and "robot/A.I. sex" is fast becoming popular and accepted. In fact, brothels where an hour is purchased with a (highly sophisticated, A.I. equipped) "sex doll" are replacing brothels with human sex workers.

Really.

Thinking about all this is *hard*. Henry Ford once said that is why so few people do it; think. In this, he was accurate and prescient.

HOW TO PREDICT THE FUTURE BY FIRST OBSERVED MOVEMENTS OF MONEY

You could foresee the age of Siri and Alexa by observing the earliest acceptance of GPS and of online search. It was clear we would transition from an information, education and knowledge driven society to a provided, specific answer society. From "how to read maps" to "voice direct me to the nearest Starbucks." Money ran from encyclopedia to single answer providers. From reference books covering, say, "dress for success" to a YouTube video specific to "how to tie a tie."

The growing impatience of the public with learning things to know things was, as most tends are, at first evolutionary, then, now revolutionary. Money began moving to it slowly. People bought Garmin® devices, primitive GPS, for their cars as add-on devices, stuck to dashboards with suction cups. In the corporate training industry, broad-based "sales training" or "leadership training," etc. fell out of favor, replaced by micro-specific training, like "how to work with difficult people," "how to shorten the B2B sales cycle," "how to use Word." The internet then fast popularized the obtaining of micro-micro information by precise requests of search engines, and advertisers' money began moving from other media to online media, intermingling with search. These early movements of money from information and education to question-and-answer signaled the sea change in how society would deal with need or desire to do something requiring know-how. It also predicted the inevitable commoditization of know-how and devaluing of expertise and experience, which has made everything from LegalZoom.com to President Trump possible. A fine, revelatory book about this is *The Death of Expertise* by Thomas M. Nichols.

You could foresee the devastating opioid epidemic (or an equivalent of it) when President Clinton did the NAFTA deal and removed all sorts of restrictions on imports from China. The result had to be a massive explosion of permanent joblessness among America's blue collar population, and with that despair and impotent rage, domestic trauma and spouse abuse, and somehow salving the wounds; alcoholism, drug addiction, suicide. Into this fertile market came opioids; legally prescribed but in mass quantities by "pill mills" and illegally distributed as well. The book *Dopesick* by Beth Macy presents an in-depth, fact based, fascinating and terrifying examination of the rise of the opioid crisis, and is, I suggest, worth reading if for no other reason a dramatic, profound lesson in the perils of unintended consequences.

It is important to think about your customers' current spending as a pie chart, but also their future spending, in 3, 5, 7, 15 years, as pie charts, if you are to hold onto a good-sized piece of the pie.

CHAPTER 2

LOSS PREVENTION IS PROFITABLE
& Too Important to Be Left to "Operations"

"Rule #1: Don't lose money."

- Warren Buffett

In many businesses, loss prevention is a low level item. Inventory control left to an outside service, using low wage workers. Security cameras, if they exist, monitored, poorly, by *somebody* — the executives way upstairs in the C-Suite have no idea who he is, let alone ever having met him.

THIS IS MADNESS.

In many businesses, employee and vendor/deliveryman thieves' combined take equals or exceeds the pre-tax net of the owners and shareholders. And that is only the *direct* theft of cash and merchandise. It does not begin to factor in the *indirect* theft, which includes:

- **Time theft:** shopping on Amazon, working on a 'side hustle,' playing on Facebook while theoretically on the job and paid to be there. Amazon would sell 90% less goods if all employers could block access to it by their employees during working hours. That's a, pardon pun, prime reason it's so popular. If somebody is missing for an hour or two everyday while at the mall, that may get noticed. If they spend 10 minutes of every hour shopping online, who'll know?

- **Theft by willful or incompetent non-compliance** with proscribed best practices: if they drive customers away, bungle inbound calls or walk-ins, fail to provide any aspect of service as it is supposed to be performed, fail to dust and clean the service area, etc., etc. they *are* stealing and you *are* suffering losses. This is why I prescribe fully disclosed, full audio and video surveillance of every part of a business location except where the customer or patient disrobes, that A/V well monitored and used in coaching the coach-able and firing the rest. The most basic managerial and ownership principle is: don't expect what YOU don't inspect. God gave you two eyes so you can sleep with one open.

- **Lost customers unnoticed**. See Chapter #4.

- **Money spent absent ROI accountability**. In my bailiwick, this is advertising, marketing and promotion spend. A contribution from a guest expert, Timothy Seward of ROI REVOLUTION, on pages 127 - 142 speaks to this. Ultimately, the more going on in our business not held to live-time, on-going, ruthless accountability, the more losses occur.

None of this is below your pay grade.

Some owners and CEOs think of this in Michael Gerber/E-Myth language: working IN the business vs. ON the business. They buy it as a clear black-and-white. While it is true, as nod to Michael, that most business owners; especially small business owners spend way too much time working IN the business, actually hiding out and delighting in the minutiae. The shopkeeper stocking shelves syndrome. But the owner who never inspects the way the goods are merchandised on the shelves is an idiot. Unless and until you achieve the highest entrepreneurial achievement – replacement, and as long as you own the business, you damn well better budget some time to work IN it.

You ARE Being Robbed, And The Thieves Are Probably Laughing At You Behind Your Back

Let's go back to the outright. direct theft. Maybe getting you mad about it will get you into it.

In the supermarket and convenience store business, where I first got my in-depth education on this thanks to a client operating the largest theft control training company (based in part on his experience as an ex-deliveryman thief), there are more than 60 different ways employees steal and more than 20 ways that deliverymen steal. There are what we labeled as "Theft Tracks" that haven't changed in the 30 years passed since I worked with this company. I can still spot them easily today and know for fact that such theft is taking place. Most owners of these businesses deny this reality. I saw it proved without exception, with hundreds of these businesses, from large chains to small mom 'n pops. The thieves get more than the owners' net. **If half is diligently stopped and that money re-captured, the advertising and marketing budget can be doubled without dipping into net profit, and *that's* alchemy.** Don't zip by that. Buying growth, speed of growth, competitive advantage requires finding money to do it with. If you do that with capital raise or debt, you encumber the business. Soon, it's an athlete trying to run with a piano strapped to his back. If you liberate the money from within its ordinary flow through the business, you perform alchemy and can buy growth without being indebted one way or another to some 3rd parties who become heavier and heavier burdens.

This is not unique to the C-store and grocery industry. A few years back, I worked for three years with one of the top expense reduction consulting firms exclusively serving hospitals. I quickly realized many of the same thefts were occurring. Different, additional ones too. But, as example, hospitals were and are actually, unforgivably letting drug company reps stock the locked room shelves with their drugs. While in there, they can swipe a few bottles of other drugs. Under-deliver but count in theirs. Single pills have high black market value. This is the same way the bread deliveryman robs the C-store. Hospitals also have the equivalent of C-stores inside them, and they get robbed by both deliverymen and employees just as the 7-11 at the corner does. Vendor, employee and collusive vendor-employee theft is a factor in EVERY business.

Assume you have 9 employees and, by varied means, not even thinking of their actions as criminal, they each steal just $5.00 a day. That's roughly $1,250.00 a year x 9 = $11,250.00. Not deadly. You probably won't even notice. Of course, over 20 years it's $225,000.00 that could have been used as free growth capital or gone into your retirement savings. But add a zero, which is the more likely number. Now it's $2.2-MILLION. Or, if you have 18 employees, $4.4-MILLION. You get the idea – but you'll fight it tooth 'n nail …

Not In MY House. MY Employees Would NOT Steal From ME. Our Vendors Are Honest And Trustworthy Or We Wouldn't Have Them.

The ravings of fools.

But if you must indulge such belief, at least follow Reagan's advice: Trust – but verify. Or Maverick's: Trust – but always cut the cards.

As I was finishing this chapter, news broke locally, where I live, about the Cleveland Clinic losing $2.2-Million by embezzlement, by one employee in accounting, successfully prosecuted and, after 3 years' tug of war, finally sentenced and sent to prison. I imagine everybody views the catch and clobbering of this embezzler as a victory. It should strike fear. A principle of mine is: there's never one cockroach. If you see one skittering across the floor and crush it with your boot, your next act better be prying loose all the baseboards with a crowbar. One seen, 100 or 1,000 concealed. If their "system" has holes one "cockroach" could exploit for $2.2-Million, catching him does not fix those holes. Further, it suggests the bigger problem of attitude, i.e. lack of vigilance, promising more, different kinds of holes.

Same week, local news also featured a community's Toys For Tots facility robbed of all the valuable toys, notably electronic devices, by its own seasonal workers/volunteers, because they were given keys to the place to come in and work at odd hours, and there were no surveillance cameras. Turned out, a group of thieves took the jobs to do the heist. Toys from impoverished tots. (Reference the plot of *Bad Santa*.)

For the record, human nature works as follows: there are 5% of the people who are hard-wired so they cannot lie, cheat or steal. 5% hard-wired to lie, cheat and steal all the time, even if there's no advantage. That 5%, by the way, can often sail through honesty assessments and lie but pass lie detector tests. In between, <u>the other 90%, you and me included, live by situational ethics. We need three conditions present to steal</u>:

1: Need or Perceived Need
2: Ability To Rationalize
3: Opportunity To Go Undetected.

<u>*Need*</u> and <u>*Ability To Rationalize*</u> are subjective and ebbs and flows. A long honest employee, low-ranking or high-ranking, may abruptly face new and dire need: opioid addiction, gambling debts spiraled out of control, costly mistress, and so on. The ability to justify theft is also subjective and relatively easy – like: *I do all the real work and the bosses take all the money, take vacations I can't afford, and besides, they'll never miss a ream of paper now and then for my side hustle, a few doughnuts eaten and not paid for, a battery for my dead broke sister's car.* The only thing that can be controlled is (perception of) opportunity to go undetected. FACT: If you aren't aggressive and visible and effective at that, you are being robbed. A lot.

Everything in that paragraph applies to the indirect thefts, too. The sales rep who refuses to use your phone script and "freelances" is engaged in *criminal* activity that may expose you to liability and/or lost sales. If he has Need, Ability to Rationalize and Opportunity To Go Undetected, he'll be miles away from your script in short order. Guaranteed. (If he has a better script, he should bring it forward, get permission to split-test and prove it, it should become THE script for all sales reps, and he should get a bonus. If he uses it surreptitiously, in defiance of your proscribed script, he should be caught and frogmarched out of the building as a criminal, fired.)

These kinds of acts of deviance and malfeasance are as varied as there are people on the planet. I have uncovered many in every business I've ever consulted with, when given the opportunity to hunt for them and reveal them. If you refuse to define them, police against them and coach adherence to them, you will have "quiet anarchy" throughout your business – at great cost.

Anarchy is evolutionary before it becomes revolutionary. Google, for example, has permitted its beginnings with its employees – first with petitions and internal intra-net rallying against doing work for the U.S. military; permitting conservatives or Trump supporters to even be there; sexism in hiring and pay, etc. Next came, mass employee walk-outs. Soon, all-out "Lord Of The Flies."

Anarchy and alchemy can't live in the same house.

Which brings us back to my closed loop: if you move dollars recaptured by loss prevention, essentially money sneaking out the back door, around to the front door, bumping up ad and marketing investment, you perform alchemy. You have made marketing dollars materialize out of thin air. You can out-spend competitors for customer acquisition and retention without denting gross or net margins. They play with one set of economics but you get to play with another. If all NFL teams but yours were rigidly salary capped but you could spend 4X more, and they were limited to 22 man rosters but you could have 60, who wins? Unless you are unbelievably incompetent, your team is invincible.

LOSS PREVENTION IS A PROFIT CENTER, NOT AN EXPENSE

(Invest Accordingly)

1% of Gross lost by stolen office supplies, personal use of company's FedEx account, copying the church bulletins on the company's copier, etc. – but it's *only 1%*.

1% lost by stolen merchandise walking out the back door. *Only 1%*.

1% lost by "freebies" given to friends, family. *1%*.

1% lost to vendors' over-billing and under-delivering and/or by deliveryman theft.

1% lost to outright embezzlement.

Just 5% of gross. EQUALS what % of pre-tax net? In many businesses 33% of pre-tax net. That's without factoring in time theft and losses by non-compliance and defiance. That may raise the losses to 10% of gross = 66% of the available profit. **Do you want LOSS as your equal partner?**

CHAPTER 3

THE ACTIONABLE ESSENCE
Test And Split-Test, As Fast As You Can

"If I had to live my life again, I'd make the same mistakes, only sooner."

- Tallulah Bankhead, actress (1903-1968)

KNOWLEDGE
IS **NOT** POWER.

You've been told your entire life that it is. The big lie of a university education is that, by knowledge gained, proved by diploma, you hold power. Over $1-Trillion of college debt has been run up on this fraudulent premise. Books, courses, seminars are also sold by this premise; that somehow just reading or listening or attending will imbed new knowledge and that will make you more powerful. Corporations invest fortunes in mining, collecting and organizing data, presented in spreadsheets and pie charts and power points presentations, in the belief that data, i.e. knowledge is power. All of this is *nonsense*.

Only data that can and will be productively and profitably used can provide power. Only information that can and will be constructively used can provide power.

Applied knowledge is power. Knowledge is not.

To do successful financial engineering in and for a business, we need all the relevant factual information *we can use* that we can get, as fast, and as cheaply as we can get it. We can't afford distractions and detours, meandering into the gathering of information we can't or won't use. We can't let people obfuscate vital truths with gigantic fog banks of information. We must get to *the essence*.

The essence is: <u>sales</u>. The great ad man David Ogilvy defined good advertising as: advertising that sells. With this, he annoyed all his peers and staff in his own agency, because the relationship between ad agencies and clients is deliberately kept in a fog bank. But, in advertising, there is a perfect opportunity for gaining knowledge that can be practically and quickly applied, to increase sales.

One of the best sources of useful information comes from my world of direct-response advertising and direct marketing: the split test.

An Example: Sequence Reversal

Years back, when I was a boozer, I often ordered "Chivas Regal and water with a lemon twist," but 80%+ of the time got only the Chivas Regal and water, and had to send the wait-person back for a lemon peel. The simplest of split-tests --- sequence reversal --- delivered the remedy: when I ordered "a lemon peel twist … (pause) … with Chivas Regal and water," I got what I ordered 80% of the time. I also found my odds of getting this right were substantially higher if I was the last person at the table to order, next best if first, but hopeless if second or third, in the middle (having to do with primacy and recency).

The actual results from a split-test of two different ways of ordering the same beverage *dictated* the best of the two to use moving forward, to get the best possible result. This is important. How I wanted to order, what others with me thought of the way I ordered, what the cocktail waitress thought (and if she was offended or irritated) – none of that was relevant, if I was after the best result.

A simple marketing example: we create two different offer pages for the same website. Each has three price option packages, from most expensive labeled as Best Value to middle labeled to Better Value to lowest priced labeled Good Value. On one page, the Best Value is first, at top of stack, then Better, than Good last, at bottom of the stack. On the other page, it is reversed, Good first, on top; Better; Best last, at bottom. Everything else is the same. For a day or a week, we drive a lot of traffic to these order pages through the same sales website from the same, single source. We flip-flop the traffic, so half winds up at one order page, half at the other. If the stacking of highest priced to lowest vs. lowest to highest or vice versa is going to make any significant difference, in short order, we will *know*.

More importantly, we will be able to immediately apply our newfound knowledge in a practical, productive and profitable way.

We don't need focus groups, industrial psychologists, refugees from academia moonlighting as communication experts, committees, studies published in *Harvard Business Review*. We don't need months or calendar quarters. Everybody can shut up about their opinions. We'll *know*. And we can then apply this *know-ing* in practical ways. Not assembled opinions. Facts.

In a book *108 PROVEN SPLIT-TEST WINNERS* by Russell Brunson, a "student" of mine, and one of the truly brilliant entrepreneurs focused on online media, I am given credit for a particular type of offer winning a split test. You can see it on Page 26. In a different set of circumstances, this very same test could have turned out the other way around, mine as the loser. Not often. Most times, mine wins. *But <u>not</u> always.* That's why opinions can't count. Not collective, consensus opinions. Not expert opinions. Not even MY opinions – and let's be clear, mine are a lot better than most ☺. Alchemy is done with facts.

Split-tests reveal facts. Reveal useable, certain truth. This is hard to come by, by other means.

This same exercise can be done with every split-testable element throughout a business' advertising and marketing. And it should be.

But it need not stop there.

As with my lemon twist and Chivas example, lots of things can be split-tested, in recruiting and hiring, in staff training, in store layout, in sales process, just about everything. **As much as possible, as often as possible, you want to be making decisions and setting policy based on "Which works better – this or that?"** In this way, you replace opinion and belief and bias with fact. Subjectivity with objectivity. And you get opportunities to act for immediate impact.

You don't want to fill shelves with binders of information or have long-winding meetings discussing information. You want to act on information, and to do so, you need to focus on getting (only) information you can act on.

This is alchemy. It is turning knowledge into action and information into gold. Not knowledge into knowledge and information into information.

Consultants – and I am one – typically love doing surveys and polls, research, compiling data and information and then delivering it in fancy-pants presentations full of pie charts and bar graphs, or at meetings with power point presentations their team spent weeks assembling. I do not do this. I am about the *actionable essence*, not the elegant, impressive presentation. French restaurants are all about the presentation – but there's never much to eat. Some friends, my wife and my then young daughter were once evicted from such a restaurant because we couldn't stop laughing at the tuxedoed waiters' revealing, with grand flourish, such teeny tiny food. The old Wendy's ad slogan applies: *where's the beef?*

As I was working on this chapter, a reasonably rational, intelligent client, CEO of a mid-sized company, presented me with new data about his customers' attitudes, converted by consultants to a "score-board." In 3 months, their score had gone up by 20 points. He and his team and the consultants all had a pat-each-other-on-the-back, high fives celebratory lunch. He was super enthusiastic with this accomplishment. I guess it's fine. Reminds me of people who compete in horse shows, at great cost, to win *ribbons*. I own race-horses. We compete in races to win money. So I asked: how are you going to convert this data into cash? What cash comes from the 20 point rise? What are you doing differently and quickly to capitalize on this happy result? *Where's the beef?* When do we eat?

My questions were not well received. I was peeing on the parade.

An Alchemist's Question

Here is an alchemist's question, whenever information is about to be presented to you by anybody in any form, but especially by your own internal people or by consultants:

> "Wait. Stop.
> Once I have the information
> you are about to give me,
> how am I going to be able to act on it
> – for profit?"

If there's no good answer, it's <u>not</u> good information. In other words, get the possible actions enunciated first, then let the information consume time and attention. This is exactly the opposite of the way most executives, business owners, and others operate. They take in new, served up information like some undiscerning glutton eats anything and everything served up at a buffet. They take in new information and then try to figure out IF it might be useful and actionable, and if so, how. Enormous amounts of time are wasted by this backasswards practice.

This is how you can train and discipline yourself and others to stop wading around in superfluous information and focus on *profitable* information.

Here is an analogy of the importance of this. Two men, both with high risk of stroke or heart attack. One has clearly labeled bottles of aspirin strategically placed throughout his home and office so he can quickly get an aspirin or two to chew and swallow, or someone else present could do so for him. The other has large 5-pound coffee cans, each containing a mix of some aspirin tablets, some M&Ms, some coffee beans, some Rolaids® lozenges, some marbles, some gravel, and some thumbtacks. Which man, suddenly and abruptly in need of an aspirin survives? This is the difference between getting only information and knowledge that can be profitably applied versus getting some such information all mixed up with a lot more, varied information items for which you have no practical use.

Alchemy requires focus and *focused effort*. In its mythical context, alchemy was about one thing and one thing only: turning ordinary metals into gold. Not into silver or water or oil. Not turning oats or wildflowers or mud into gold. Focus. Focused effort. Real alchemy in business mirrors this. It is about turning actionable information into action and profitable information into profit. That and that alone. Period.

Candidly, those of us in the information business have a self-interest agenda somewhat in conflict with this. Most advisors, consultants, coaches, experts, authors, speakers, publishers do not want to be asked the above alchemy question. We actually prosper by organizing herds of vociferous *consumers of* information, not discerning, discriminate and demanding *users of* information who insist on receiving only information that can be used. If you are going to do knowledge alchemy, turning information into gold, you have to be wary of us! There, I said it.

DAN KENNEDY'S OFFER WINNING A SPLIT TEST

from *"108 Proven Split Test Winners"*

BY RUSSELL BRUNSON

BACKEND TESTS

Real tests of webinars, closings, sales processes and more to increase how often customers buy.

THE "DAN KENNEDY" OFFER

♛ *Dan Kennedy Style Offer*

> **Give Smarter Webinar a Shot Today and Save For a Lifetime! PLUS, Keep All Twenty Presentations Just For Trying!!!**
>
> **Special Price**
> ~~$67/month~~
> only **$47/month**
>
> **Get Started Now!**
>
> *REMEMBER: As a thank you for giving Smarter Webinar a try, you get to keep the 20 presentations, scripts, and promotional sequences that are currently loaded into the system — even if you decide not to stay with the service!*

Test by Mike Cooch

One of my friends, Mike Cooch from LocalIncomeLabs. com, sent us a really cool test that I wanted to show you because the only real "tweak" was the actual offer. Sometimes we focus so much on the little tests, that we forget the biggest thing we can change (that will often have the biggest impact) is our offer. Check out the huge increase Mike saw by tweaking his offer:

We just re-launched Smarter Webinar, a $47/month automated webinar service to our list. We took two approaches and did a little split test:

- **Promo #1:** Sell a valuable, low end offer ($19 for 20 done for you webinar presentations, email scripts, etc.), then sell Smarter Webinar as the upsell with the offer to discount the first month. So the total they paid today was only $47, the normal cost of one month of Smarter Webinar.

- **Promo #2:** Sell Smarter Webinar directly, but offer same 20 webinar presentations as an "amazing free gift" just for trying the service" (Dan Kennedy style

Here are the results:

Promo #1: $6.25 EPC
- Recurring Smarter Webinar accounts sold: 34
- Total Revenue: $3,441
- Total Recurring Revenue: $1,598

Promo #2: $8.64 EPC
- Recurring Smarter Webinar accounts sold: 153
- Total Revenue: $7,191
- Total Recurring Revenue: $7,191

I guess we know the right way to promote continuity to list! Even if we see much more churn from the Promo #2 buyers, we are going to come out way ahead.

TOTAL REVENUE

109% increase

$3,441
Low End Offer
With Upsell

$7,191
"Dan Kennedy"
Style Offer

BELIEVE NOTHING,

no matter where you read it

or who has said it,

not even if I have said it,

unless it agrees with

your own reason

and your own common sense.

— BUDDHA —

CHAPTER 4

Relentless
FOLLOW-UP
Marketing

"Wanna fly, you got to give up the shit that weights you down."

- Toni Morrison

THERE ARE (ONLY) TWO BASIC KINDS OF BUSINESS CULTURES **PICK WISELY.**

One is very fragile. The other is *anti-fragile*. The decision about which kind of company you want and will insist on having leads to thatched hut on shifting sand or rock solid fortress atop a high, rocky mountain.

One is: sales. The other is: marketing. There are many differences between the two, but the biggest is that the first is always awash in waste. Gargantuan waste. Of ad dollars, leads, customers. This is so because salespeople are negligent and lousy at follow-up. They are lazy about it, but worse they resist it because they – and often those up the food chain above them in their company – *don't actually believe in it*. If you depend on humans doing selling, you'll drift to depending on salespeople to do follow-up; they won't, and that leaves your business fragile.

This is a little realized truth. Yet it is on display if we look.

I want to be very, very clear on this point: your company may be INFECTED with a bias against follow-up that costs you an enormous, but mostly unknown and unquantifiable amount of money. You *can't* know what you *didn't* get but could have, if you weren't relying on sales culture and sales people.

Sales Culture Businesses are controlled by a secular religion, colloquially expressed as "*there ain't no Be-Backs*," meaning if you fail to close the sale with the prospect at the sales appointment, that prospect is dead to you after he leaves. This religion can be found in iron-fisted control of the automobile sales business, the financial advisor business, dental practices, and many, many others. I've encountered it with clients in health care, in the hearing aid business; with the largest weight loss company in the United States; and in my own field of information marketing, i.e. consulting, coaching, published resources. Further, **disbelief in the value of unconverted leads runs rampant**. Despite the empirical evidence in most commerce categories that 7 to 21 sequential interest and trust building contacts are behind 80% of all eventual sales, and evidence that even in fast decision oriented businesses --- like a DUI or PI law practice --- over half of all sales are made to slow maturing buyers, nobody believes the facts, and nobody wants to manage comprehensive follow-up over months. Their culture is quite primitive. *Eat what you kill today, kill today or don't eat.*

This is always wrong.

It is ignorant. Willfully denying of facts. In the way. Costly. *Wrong*.

If you permit a Sales Culture, a "today is the only day" culture to infect or rule your company and its sales team – or yourself – you eat only hard fought for crumbs, when you leave untouched a bountiful feast. Also, you eat well only in very good times. In poor times, when buyers with money are scarce, the failure inherent in your approach becomes painfully evident, but it will probably be too late to fix it before starving.

Buffett says: you never really know who's "naked" until the tide goes out. For "naked" substitute: stupid, lazy, feckless, disorganized, financially inefficient. Dependent on methodology that only works in good times – when, bluntly, *any* methodology works. Sales Culture is the business equivalent of an emperor with no clothes; naked, without system or process.

As dumb as this is, 80% of all businesses, small and large, have primitive Sales Cultures, relying only on what can be captured by manual labor hunting and killed each day for their survival. **They may be up to their ass in modern tech, but they are run by people with caveman minds**. Here we are, at a time of unprecedented ease in implementing complex and sophisticated marketing systems, still acting as if it was 1960, with victory dependent on having the fastest, strongest, brawniest, most determined silver-tongued beasts sent out to fetch.

Relentless Follow-Up Marketing has never been easier, more easily automated. Never been cheaper to do. Never has so much sophisticated message-to-market match by list/lead segmentation been possible. Yet, there's less of it than when it was difficult and costly, before email, Facebook and Facebook re-targeting, Instagram, webinars, automated mail sequences, and technology like Infusionsoft, HubSpot, and similar platforms and tools. There's no reason now --- *only excuses* --- for failing at Relentless Follow-Up Marketing.

By the way, rarely does being good at making excuses and making money go together.

So, let's back up, then ultimately I'll use the hearing aid and the financial advisor businesses as examples. We'll back up, and lay the foundation for getting this right.

Door #1 Or Door #2?

Backing up, there are two kinds of companies, organizations and businesses. There are Sales Culture Businesses, where all the heavy lifting is to be done by salespeople during a sales appointment. Success is dependent on selling over and past skepticism, resistance and fear … overcoming objections … and hard closing the sale. In businesses of this Culture, little is done to more gently prepare the prospect to buy in advance of the sales appointment and even less – *often nothing* – is done to patiently and persistently stay with the prospects who escape the sales appointments without buying. As I said, this describes 80% of all businesses, so if you are seeking competitive advantage you can start by *not* doing this. (Yes, *the majority*; the majority in your industry are dead ass wrong.)

Given what we know today, sticking with this business model is like refusing to travel because of the flat earth. Given the technology and tools available today, it is akin to farming with mule and walk-behind plow. If this is the way you are running your business, *shame on you.*

There are Marketing Culture Businesses where the sales appointment and the salesperson conducting it are just *one part of a process* incorporating thoroughly preparing the prospect to buy without resistance in front of the sales appointment and Relentless Follow-Up after the appointment with the prospects who did not buy. There is a term for this: *sophisticated.* The difference is graphically depicted on the next page. The pre-sales appointment matter is dealt with in Chapter 5. Here, we'll stick with the follow-up after the "failed" sales appointment.

Change Your Math, Change Your Business
A Money Math Fact That Should Not Be Ignored

The reason you want to replace Sales Culture with Marketing Culture and primitive selling with sophisticated marketing+selling is very simple in financial terms: you do *not* pay just for your buyers. You pay for every lead, every prospect, every phone call, every website visit, every walk-in and every appointment. Whatever the closing percentage is, there is always a lot of bought and paid for prospects wasted with a Sales Culture. Pressed on who owns responsibility for comprehensive and relentless follow-up, no one can be found. You are paying for opportunities never utilized.

Often, a business owner can tell me his Cost Per Sale. If his advertising and marketing budget is $10,000.00 for a month and he achieves 20 sales of his products or services, he'll assign an average of $500.00 to his CPS. If he's a deeper thinker, he'll also divide his overhead by 20, calculate the commissions paid to salespeople, and possibly factor in some other expenses. But paying too much attention to the CPS alone is extremely deceptive, even if it is a "good" number. You can see if you are generating revenue per sale above the CPS, on average, and transaction by transaction, but this does not reveal anything about your financial efficiency.

In a sales culture business, the owner doesn't even know this math, because it is concealed inside the efforts (and non-efforts) and activities and costs of his sales team.

To measure financial efficiency, we need to work backwards, to consider CPA and CPL. CPA = Cost Per Appointment, CPL = Cost Per Lead. And, obviously, % of leads converted to appointments, then % of appointments converted to sales. These are among the most truly important "money math" numbers, and your CFO or your CPA are very unlikely to focus on them. Your sales people are extremely unlikely to tell you the truth about them.

(A complete look at money math numbers can be found in Chapter 46 of my book *No B.S. Ruthless Management of People and Profits,* 2nd Edition.)

Looking at CPL, if his $10,000.00 ad and marketing spend generates 50 inbound requests for information via whatever means – phone, website, etc. – he has, on the surface a $200.00 CPL. If it generates 500, he has a $20.00 CPL. Either way, the % of leads converted to appointments is the first internal spot where financial efficiency may be good or bad, and may be subject to a lot of improvement if worked on.

Consider this large advertiser I worked with, with several offices of a professional practice in a community. They invested about $100,000.00 a month in advertising, marketing, PR, and the costs of the main staff person in each office fielding calls from prospective patients and that generated about 2,000 leads a month: CPL of $50.00. Because at the end of all the sausage making, they were getting 30 to 40 new patients a month at an average value of $15,000.00 each, with a 30% net profit, they were roughly +$60,000.00; nearly +$750,000 a year, *and happy, happy, happy*. But in-depth examination revealed gross inefficiency, with only about 100 (5%) converted to appointments, thus a CPA of $1,000.00. All I had to do to double their net profit was move that needle from 100 appointments per 2,000 leads to 150 with no increase in front end ad or marketing spend and a little spend back-end, after failed sales appointments. Certain expenses stayed level. We just did a lot more with the lead flow they had (in defiance of their secular religious beliefs about their non-buyers and their superhuman salespeople).

Leaving This Up To Salespeople Defies The 'Math' Of Human Behavior

In *any* organized population – such as a sales team – 1% are great, 4% damn good, 15% adequate, 40% barely okay if you're generous in defining 'okay,' and 40% feckless and useless to others or themselves. No group is comprised of 1%'ers. Not even of 1%'ers and 4%'ers. Plus, human performance varies day to day by life and mood. *Most humans suck* at most tasks and responsibilities, but they really, really suck at Relentless Follow-Up.

To scale sales-related financial efficiency by getting better and higher productivity per human salesperson is nearly impossible. Most sales-forces divide up just like any other closed population, again: only 1% great, 4% good, 15% adequate, 40% barely adequate, 40% useless. You can keep churning 'n burning the bottom 40% or even the bottom 80%, but overall, ultimately, you are not going to materially improve any of them beyond their own performance levels. Some companies squeeze more juice by re-drawing geographic territories, by routing best leads and best accounts to best performers, and by other means of lead flow management. Still, you can only squeeze the salespeople so much. And if the size of your sales team grows, you'll find the average productivity of each salesperson declines. It becomes harder and harder to keep cleansing the lowest producers because there are so many slots to keep filled, so owner-manager tolerance for barely adequate productivity increases. Gradually this dampens results by shrinking expectations. Thus, the motto: When All Else Fails – Lower Your Expectations.

For the record, training and motivation are *not* scaleable either. I've been in and around those fields my entire life. Training only helps those eager and willing to learn and work at using it: 1%, definitely, 4% probably, 15% maybe. External motivation by pep talk, deeper personal development, incentives, contests and competition only works with the self-motivated. 1% certainly, always, 4% probably, episodically, 15% maybe. You can have 'em doing energy yells, walking on hot coals, etc. all you want. You can worship "business culture" put happy posters on every wall, trek off to leadership retreats in the woods, and bring in team-building shamans. It'll wind up 1%, 4%, 15%. I'm *not* against most of the motivation stuff, mind you. But it is all a means of supporting the top 20%, not transfiguring the entire performance pyramid. And if you must choose between investing in attempts to "pump up your people" OR strengthen your process, put the money in the process.

Not only aren't people scaleable, but the opposite usually occurs. There's an old Michael Keaton movie about clones. The first one is nearly a perfect clone. The second one has some problems. By the time there's a #5, he's drooling, stumbling and can't feed himself. Cloning yourself or your #1 is just not viable. That's why giant companies that must have huge numbers of humans at work typically have them laboring, not selling; flipping the burgers, not selling the franchises. And why AI and robots is such a seductive, popular idea that big employers are investing in it lustfully.

The thing that can be scaled, because it can be done *by systems* in place of humans, is marketing-related financial efficiency, notably by squeezing a lot more juice out of your leads, in front of and after the sales appointment attempt. In other words, **the more you can separate achieving maximum possible value from your leads from the performance of your human salespeople, the more you can improve your business' financial efficiency.**

Conversely, the more dependent squeezing maximum value from leads is dependent on squeezing better performance out of salespeople, the more frustrated you'll be trying to boost financial efficiency.

Further, even if you boost results by, essentially, horse-whipping the salespeople, the result will be *temporary*. Your whip arm will get tired. If you try carrots instead, those results are temporary. Today's incentive is tomorrow's entitlement. But when you boost results by building, implementing and automating better Relentless Follow-Up MARKETING and other systems, positive results can be permanent.

This is true in both small businesses and giant companies with large inside and/or field sales organizations. Either way, if you put prospects made more likely to buy by the marketing before the sales appointment in front of one or one thousand salespeople (and reduce the number of sales appointment time slots filled with ill-prepared, skeptical, resistant and difficult to close prospects), you will get more return on your investment in each salesperson – from the superstars all the way down to the barely adequate. You can even make 15%'ers get the results of 4%'ers and 4%'ers get the results of 1%'ers.

There are many ways to achieve this, and some seem counter-intuitive. For example, this may be accomplished by deliberately spending MORE per lead and MORE per appointment in order to screen out the lowest quality (likelihood of buying) prospects and fill your appointments with the highest quality prospects. If the quality of the prospect increases the average close rate by 10% and/or drives price/fee elasticity by 10%, spending more on CPL and CPA could yield disproportionately higher revenues and profits overall and per salesperson.

For the small business with either its owner or just one key person conducting sales presentations --- like the dentist doing new patient case presentations --- this becomes vital, because there is a fixed limit on the number of sales appointment slots that exist. If, for example, only 30 sales presentations can be made in a month the highest financial efficiency will come from effecting those sales appointments in every productive way possible, by prospect screening and selection, by pre-appointment marketing, and by post-appointment follow-up with non-buyers – not leaving that up to the salesperson.

So, here are all the ways we might positively impact the value of each sales appointment/attempt, other than having better salespeople and/or better sales management:

1. In advance of sales appointment:

The better prepared a prospect is in advance – to be receptive, respectful, trusting – the less the sale depends on the attitude and applied aptitude of the inherently unreliable and variably performing sales person, the more able your business is to get good results from more prospects without superstar salespeople, and often, even, the less the salespeople need to be paid per sale. I have just described enormous financial efficiency. For details, see Chapter #5.

2. At sales appointment:

Physical environment matters. Choreography matters. Often, a lot of money has been invested in getting a prospect to a store, showroom, office, clinic or other location only, there, to sell in poor conditions.

3. After "failed" sales appointment - relentless follow-up:

Follow-up after a failed selling attempt will produce subsequent sales from no less than 5% to as much as 20% of the non-buyers. Period. No exceptions. I have proven this in hundreds of different environments, situations and businesses, with the sales attempt occurring online, on inbound call. By outbound call, by in home appointment, by in store or showroom appointment, by any means, any place, B2C or B2B.

Assume for the sake of this conversation you could do all three of these and each improved sales conversions by a paltry 1%. 3% from all. If your present conversion rate is 10%, this boosts the value of each and every sales appointment by 30%. (Yes just to 13%, but for those who went to public school, from 10 to 13 is a 30% increase.)

Now, let's get to my hearing aid and financial advisor examples, just for the third area of opportunity ...

With a client company in the hearing aid industry, with over 1,000 offices, I was candidly successful at getting less than 50 to implement a multi-step, direct-mail and email Appointment, No Sale Follow-Up Marketing System. 90% resisted it because of secular religion, fear of taking pressure off of the salespeople to close hard, stupidity about ROI math, sloth and incompetence. But of the relative few who did use it, the average results from the follow-up were 15% of the prospects who left their appointments without buying came back within the 6 weeks of the System's application to them, and another 5% came back over the next 12 months to buy, referring to the follow-up as the reason they returned. On every 100 appointments, this represents about **a $120,000.00 rescue of revenue that would otherwise be lost i**n whole or large part. Without the System, follow-up on these prospects who – by the salesperson's attitude – failed to buy at their appointments would be left to those salespeople blaming the "bad" prospect for not immediately buying. This is Hillary Clinton Thinking: her election loss due to the failure of the electorate; their stupidity, the men's gender bias against women, wives' domination by their husbands thus voting against their best interests, etc.; "the deplorables."

Blaming the "deplorable" non-buyer is rarely a productive idea.

$120,000.00 of lost or extra revenue per 100 appointments is a lot. Had the company gotten wholeheartedly behind this and forced its franchise owners and its corporate store managers to utilize the System, as much as $48-Million of extra revenue existed to be collected. (And royalties for lil' ol' me of as much as 7% of that; $3.4-Million that I never saw ☹.) To put $48-million in perspective, the giant Walgreen's corporation announced late in 2018 a Herculean re-structuring plan featuring arguably severe and draconian cost-cutting measures, fraught with peril, to try and book $300-million in a year. The $48-million available by my method has *no* peril. They're doing bloody, side effect laden surgeries. I was doing alchemy.

Next example: I was brought in to train and coach a group of financial advisors, all already earning no less than $250,000.00 a year, most twice that or better, therefore all *not* dumb, and high performing. Yet at the very first meeting, I got a stunningly dumb answer to a basic question. And this is the thing about humans: even demonstrably smart ones do remarkably dumb things. *A lot.*

Their #1 business model is advertising and using direct-mail to fill "free dinner workshops" with 50+ people holding significant money in 401k or other retirement accounts. At the workshops, after doing their best dog 'n pony show, they sign up as many of those prospects as possible for private appointments. The best book 60% to 70%, the average is 40% to 50%, therefore a lot hit only 20% to 30%. So there are no less than 30 out of 100 to as many as 80 out of 100 "left-overs." Keep in mind that these prospects --- thought of by many advisors in much the same way the hearing aid salespeople and operators thought of their non-buyers --- took the time and trouble to read advertising, decide to do something they probably didn't relish doing, register and by doing so provide their contact information, get in their car, and come to a workshop. *So I asked: what do y'all do with the left-overs?*

Three answers, all three stunningly stupid.

One, nothing. *Nothing!*

Two, we keep them on the mail and email lists "for a while," mostly causing them to be re-invited to the same workshop they were already at. Even if you are Stevie Wonder, you should be able to see that makes *no* sense. (Note: you MUST learn and use list/lead and unconverted lead segmentation.)

Three, if Helen has time, Helen calls them and tries to get them to book an appointment. Of course, since Helen hates this task equal in her mind to cleaning up backyard dog shit with her bare hands, and since she's no good at it, how often do you think Helen has time for this? The over-under is zero.

Re. #2 and #3, I offer advice from both Deming and Buffett: if it's worth doing, it's worth doing in the most effective way possible. If it's not worth doing in the most effective way possible, it's well worth not doing at all. In this case, I can prove it's worth doing as effectively as possible.

We implemented an Attend Workshop, No Appointment System, with 16 follow-up steps, 6 mail, 10 email, over 4 weeks, getting sterner as it progressed, all driving to the appointment. The average results virtually mirrored those described above for the hearing aid offices, but in dollars they were worth 50% to 100% more.

No-Fail Follow-Up

An old, I imagine out of print book I got early in my business life is W. Clement Stone's *The Success System That NEVER FAILS*. That is one heck of a title. A bit of hyperbole, but in essence, the book delivers. It is also one of those aspirational titles, worth having around just to see the cover. Its challenge is a damn good one: **DO YOU HAVE SUCH A SYSTEM? Can you diagram it for me? Prove it is being adhered to 100% of the time?**

Fact is, few business leaders ever really attempt *this*. They build, buy, operate and settle for quasi systems known in advance to involve tolerance of some amount of episodic failure. Point: whatever ill you tolerate, you get more of.

It is possible to have *no-fail* follow-up. A prescribed, largely pre-built, largely automated series of follow-up steps and communications applied to each and every lead or prospect or customer on a locked in schedule – this happens on Day 3, this on Day 5, this on Day 8, etc. The above described system for the financial advisors required only the entry of the names and addresses of workshop attendees not booking appointments the next A.M., then software and vendors took over, pre-written pieces were auto-populated with each prospect's name and information, and a high level of reliability and consistency ensued. Mostly, Helen would do that first step of the data entry because it freed her from being asked to do far more onerous things and enduring her boss' occasional temper tantrums when he realized no follow-up was occurring. You can get *this* done. *It* is scalable.

This is what I do, for clients. I replace sales culture with marketing culture, dependency on humans with reliance on systems. If sales people are kept involved, they are integrated, they are "money math managed," they are provided opportunity to experience much greater success with less stress – if *they'll get with the program*. (Typically, about 1/3rd will, 2/3rds won't, and good riddance to 'em. We can hope they land at your competitors.) Sometimes, fewer or even no sales people are needed after all the marketing systems are put in place. Either way, the business is transformed from fragile to anti-fragile.

FAILURE TO FULLY MONETIZE

I had the Stanley Steemer® guys out to clean my house's air ducts and carpets. Two of them. There for almost 5 hours. One did upsell the protectant after cleaning, so points for that. Total tab: $1,670.90, plus $200 tips. **But here's what** *didn't* **happen:**

FAILURE#1: <u>NO</u> ATTEMPT to book next cleaning in 6, 8 or 12 months.

FAILURE #2: <u>NO</u> ATTEMPT to enroll in monthly auto-pay for bundle of services throughout year.

FAILURE #3: <u>NO</u> ATTEMPT to sell air purifier, humidifier or water purifier or, better, arrange a sales appointment for a rep highly skilled in selling those to come out and do a demo.

FAILURE #4: <u>NO</u> ATTEMPT to leave a couple pass-along envelopes with literature and coupons, for me to give to neighbors and friends.

FAILURE #5: <u>NO</u> ATTEMPT to collect referrals.

And I watched … **FAILURE #6:** <u>NO</u> placing of "we were here at your neighbor's" door-hangers on neighboring homes' doors, to create forced referrals.

AFTER THE FACT:

FAILURE #7: <u>NO</u> thank you note, card or gift.

FAILURE #8: <u>NO</u> bounceback or tell-a-friend coupon.

Give them points for showing up, for doing fine work, and for up-selling the protectant. That makes their score a 3 out of 11. A failing grade. And that's how I look at it: they FAILED, miserably, at their opportunity to make me a repeat customer and to replicate or multiply me. FAILED. Miserably.

Let's assume by all these NO's, they sacrifice only, on average, 5% added revenue; in my case, $83.50, x 20 homes a day, x 250 days a year = $417,500.00. If you owned the company and banked all this added revenue less taxes but plus interest, in 10 years you have about $3.5-Million in your retirement account you wouldn't have otherwise. If it's a big franchisor like Stanley Steemer, multiply that added gross by, let's say, 100 market areas = $41,750,000.00 x the 7% override = $2,922,500.00 per year; $29.2-Million in 10. If this is trivial chump change to you or your company, congratulations. But for most business owners an extra several hundred thousand dollars a year *isn't*, quoting Rep. Nancy Pelosi, "crumbs." For most mid-sized companies, an extra few million dollars a year shouldn't be cavalierly ignored.

A CONFESSION, FROM THIS AUTHOR

This is an irritable book written by a perpetually irritated fellow. I have a 4-foot high cardboard cut-out of Grumpy from the Seven Dwarfs in my office bathroom, as warning to visitors. One of the things most irritating to me is utterly unnecessary waste of opportunity. I've been broke and hate seeing money wasted. If you've ever looked under every cushion and checked every pocket and still been a quarter short of a burrito at Jack In The Box and therefore gone to sleep that night hungry as I have, seeing money wasted by no cause but sheer squandering of present opportunity is *painful*. If you are guilty of such negligence, I'd like to kick you in the ass. You piss me off. If your business wastes opportunity like I've just described, when it files for bankruptcy, its demise cheers my heart. I root for your extinction.

CHAPTER #5

UP, UP, UP WE (WANT TO) GO!
Ascension Pyramids & Ladders

"Ah, but a man's reach should exceed his grasp, or what's a heaven for?"

- Robert Browning

PEOPLE WANT
UPWARD MOBILITY.

If you put it in front of them, they'll happily pay for it. This makes each customer, on average, more valuable, so you need less of them to meet the same income goals or even exceed them.

You do this with a LADDER or an ASCENSION PYRAMID.

A Ladder is square or only slightly tiered, permitting an essentially unlimited number of people to move up from one level to the next. Often, the consumer can start at any of its levels. An Ascension Pyramid (AP) has known and shown, fewer and fewer open spots on each higher level, lending itself to pre-requisites, required purchases, waiting lists, and competition by customers to move up. Either can substantially improve average customer value.

There is no greater alchemy than taking customer flow a business already has and boosting the average customer value by 2X, 5X,

10X, 20X. It is like taking the minerals in the dirt already in your backyard and turning them into gold. We're not getting a new asset. We are better and more creatively managing the assets we already have.

Russell Conwell's legendary speech and essay, his parable ACRES OF DIAMONDS was about this, conceptually and metaphysically, and it's worth finding and reading if you aren't familiar with it. I'm talking about a practical application of it. Far too much focus in business is on possible diamond fields in the distance, thus on new customer acquisition, with too little on the diamonds right in the backyard, i.e. the existing customer population. It is true that grievous damage can occur from insufficient new customer attraction. That *is* the lifeblood of the business. It should be somebody's exclusive and entire worry, and it should be on the top-5 list of DAILY concerns for the owner or CEO. But the closed loop is that the better you do with the customers you have, the more you can afford to invest in acquiring new ones. To abuse analogy, if you only pick up the diamonds laying around atop the ground, you'll go broke buying up diamond fields and mines.

How To Multiply Customer Value

There are businesses in which Ascension Pyramids are the norm. Martial arts, music and other kinds of local academies are an example. My client, Marty Fort, has two thriving music schools in the Columbia, South Carolina area, plus provides owner-operator training, coaching and support to over 1,000 other schools nationwide, most also using his Ladder of Success System® for their students. Another client, Stephen Oliver, installs this in the hundreds of martial arts academies he consults with. In my information-marketing industry, Ascension Pyramids are a norm, and can have extremely dramatic results. One such company came to me with a flat, linear sequence of purchases by its customers producing an average 3-year value of $9,000.00. Simply by re-arranging all the same products and services into an Ascension Pyramid applied to the same customers, I raised the average 3-year customer value to $34,000.00. 100 customers did equal $900,000.00, now they equal $3.4-Million. This is a 3.7 (+370%) multiple. The client can spend double what he was spending on customer acquisition AND keep a 1.7 (+170%) income boost. *That* is alchemy.

***Many* other kinds of businesses could use Ascension Pyramids or Ladders but don't**, because they don't understand them or aren't creative enough to apply the strategy in their industry where it is not a common norm. As always, industry norms are myopic and limiting. Working within them only gets incrementally better profits but never yields breakthroughs. Breakthroughs only come by defying industry norms. This should never be forgotten, broadly. Specifically, I counsel that any and every type of business should find an opportunity to create an Ascension Pyramid(s) or a Ladder(s), particularly if it *isn't* a norm in their industry.

The key reason to do it is that consumers are *pre-conditioned* to move up ladders and pyramids. We were trained in this by school, from kindergarten to university, by Scouts, by extracurricular activities, by military service and by social constructs. Your customers are basically waiting to be shown the ladder or the pyramid!

The financial efficiency purposes of getting people climbing a ladder or ascending a pyramid are:

1: Retention by ascension. Customers stay longer when they are climbing or rising from level to level, by design and aspiration, rather than static in a transactional way. If you benefit by keeping customers with you for as long as possible (and what business doesn't?), <u>one of the most productive extenders of customer tenure is their climbing from one level (of perks; of involvement; of recognition and status) to another, then another, then another.</u> If they are moving up toward a goal, they are less likely to exit. The costs attached to creating and fulfilling these higher levels are usually not proportionate to the added spend by the customers over time. The customer essentially becomes more valuable the longer he remains climbing and at higher levels, because all the original acquisition cost is amortized over more and more months or years AND the margin on higher levels' goods and services is greater than that of the initial or early or basic purchasing. This is alchemy, twice!

Let's make this elegantly simple: **if you get a customer engaged with and committed to getting to a goal** that requires him staying and spending, you can dramatically improve the staying and spending – by length, by frequency, by dollar amount(s).

2: *Forced*, greater consumption of goods and services. The online game industry is built on this: people spend huge sums on "free games" buying "extras" that help them move up from level to level. "Gamifying" all sorts of business has become 'a thing.' In the offline world, this is anything but new. I learned it as a pup in Amway. Years later, I got inside Bill Phillips' brilliant use of it, via his Body For Life customer competitions, forcing consumption of his company's nutritional supplements, drinks, and other products – with cars as top prizes. I very successfully adopted the entire template for business environments, getting a number of training, coaching and consulting companies to use it profitably. One of the best at it, true to its full, complete template is a client, Scheduling Institute, in the dental profession.

1 + 2 = Millions

When you properly combine #1 and #2 above, here's an example of what you can get:

If there are 1,000 customers who essentially stay on a flat line, moving through the same repeat or sequential purchases, let's say at average of $100.00 a month, each has a gross value of $1,200.00 a year; combined, $1.2-million per year.

But if, of the 1,000, 20%, i.e. 200 move up to a $150.00 a month level, 5%, i.e. 50 move up to a $250.00 a month level, and 1%, i.e. 10 move up to a $1,000.00 a month level, we create $1.6-million per year, i.e. $400,000.00 MORE *from the same customer base.*

10	@	$1,000.00 Month	$120,000.00 Yr.
50	@	$250.00	$210,000.00 Yr.
200	@	$150.00	$360,000.00 Yr.
740	@	$100.00/Month	$888,000.00 Yr.

$1,638,000.00

We did not have to do the difficult thing: getting a lot more customers to add the $400,000.00 of revenue. We only had to manipulate and organize the same number of customers to ascend to different levels of a pyramid.

But this only tells part of the Ascension Pyramid story.

In most situations, the upper tiers have a better/longer retention rate than the lower. Also, the upper tiers' customers tend to refer more than the lower. From a profit standpoint, the goods, services and benefits that need added for each level do not add cost proportionate to the base cost of servicing the lower level. Combine all that, and the financial efficiency of moving a customer up an Ascension Pyramid is impressive. Factoring all that in, and carrying the above example out over 5 years of retention, ascension (and attrition), we would find the $400K a year turned into $600K to $800K, and with a higher profit margin than existed with the flat line approach. The math is nearly magical.

This happens routinely in a lot of my clients' businesses. It is exactly how one, providing an Ascension Pyramid of goods and services to small businesses, grew by 10X over 5 years, turning a $5-million business into a $50-million business --- *without* needing 10X or even 3X the number of customers.

How Are Levels Created On An AP?

Most typically, the ascending value propositions for the levels of an AP rely in:

1: Bundling of goods and services / savings vs. cafeteria purchasing
2: (Greater) access to the "guru," tribe leader, owner and/or "senior" staff
3: Exclusivity
4: Status inside the community
5: Status outside the community

Here is a quick look at each:

<u>Bundling of Goods and Services</u>

#1 is the most obvious. At the very bottom of a pyramid, goods and services may be separate items with separate prices, all available or some withheld. As a customer ascends and picks the VIP Plan or Gold VIP Plan or Diamond VIP Plan, etc. goods and services get combined at some appreciable savings from their separate pricing and withheld items get added in as well. As example, you can buy just the cruise or you can buy the air travel, bookend days' hotel stay, cruise and shore excursions as a bundle, i.e. level on the pyramid. If you go up another level, you get all that bundled plus an outside cabin, early boarding and first off departure, an invitation to the captain's bon voyage party, and reserved, front table seating for all the on-board entertainment. Up another level, you get all that, but a suite in place of a stateroom, and use of a top-deck club lounge and pool apart from the riff-raff. This is pyramid shaped, because of scarcity; there are fewer outside staterooms than all staterooms but even fewer suites than outside staterooms; there is limited capacity on

VIP shore excursions; the top level's lounge and pool area is reserved for a maximum of 25. The pyramid may have 1,000 spots at the bottom, 300 at Gold, 150 at Diamond, and only 25 at Platinum.

A really interesting "trick" is that, given enough added, exclusive-to-the-high(er) levels and enough pyramid pressure from a lot fewer spots on each higher level than below, you can actually charge more for the bundle than the total of its items priced separately.

Greater Access to Guru...

#2 In many businesses, there is a "guru" or thought leader, a celebrity chef, a master jeweler; some person that customers identify with and desire access to and relationship with. The more appealing this access is, the less of it should exist at the low(er) level(s) of the pyramid, so it can be leveraged to move customers up to the higher levels.

With both #1 and #2, it's important to understand that you can create escalating, differential pricing with ever widening margins, as the costs for most of the deliverables do not rise level by level by level. This is thin air spun to gold.

Exclusivity

#3 Exclusivity, can produce a lot of price elasticity, and is easily built into pyramid levels, as I've just described in #1 and #2. The more things you concoct and offer that only a (relatively) small number of your customers can have, the better you drive ascension (if that is the only way to get those things or even to get access to those things), and the more you raise your average PROFIT per customer.

Status Inside the Community

#4 Inside the membership community of entrepreneurs that I created, and that has me as its center tent-pole (now: www.nobsinnercircle. com), there is a "bragging rights" to being at the top levels of its AP, and moving further up to my AP. This has no meaning outside the community, but a great deal of meaning in the community. Coupled with supply/demand equations that limit the number who can move up to each tier, each conferring higher in-community status, this provides significant price/fee elasticity.

Personally, as of this writing, my base consulting fee for a 7 hour private consulting day is $19,400.00, requiring trekking to my city, to meet in my home office. This is from 10X to 3X what top lawyers get to charge, and at least that multiple of what 99% of business consultants get to charge. And demand has exceeded the supply of days I'm willing to make available for more than ten consecutive years – with zero direct advertising or marketing of my services. What accounts for this high of a fee, willingly paid by more than 30 people a year? Some of the differential is because, in direct financial value, I'm a bargain even at this fee. Some of it is by specialization. But candidly, some of it is because of status gained. Almost every client comes from within the community and values status in the community. Every client wants a photo with me in "my lair," wants to take other photographs, post them to social media, and have their story(ies) of this one-on-one work day with me to tell. This allows me to inflate my fee beyond what either the billable hours or the work being done would itself support. Beyond that, most of these days lead to copywriting projects (at very high fees and royalties) or/ and Private Client Program participation, size of group strictly limited, each getting a private consulting call 10 out of 12 months, at about $35,000.00 a year. That Program is very efficient. All the calls occur on one day a month, for which I am paid about $45,000.00, 2.3X (230%) my base day rate. Being in the Private Client Program certainly has its practical benefits, but it also has in-community status.

Status Outside the Community

#5 Status outside the community can be an even stronger, more justifiable buying motive.

The publisher of this book, Forbes Books, is one of several imprints all owned and within Advantage Media Group. For some authors, one of the other imprints meets their needs to be published authors, is accessible at a lower fee*, and has less stringent content requirements and oversight. However, for some authors the status of being a Forbes book author is important, worth a higher investment*, and bears fees and costs roughly 3X (300%) higher than being published under Advantage or one of Advantage's other imprints. From a financial efficiency standpoint, Advantage's core costs for attracting an author, providing strategic and editorial support, actually publishing the book, managing distribution via Amazon, etc. do *not* multiply by 3 if using the Forbes Books identity. There is considerable financial efficiency for Advantage in moving an author up their AP to Forbes Books (if the author can qualify) and to full marketing agency service relationships. For the author utilizing his book as a centerpiece of self or business marketing*, there can also be considerable financial efficiency in these relationships with Advantage or Forbes, vs. alternative author-publisher situations.

Advantage is a hybrid book publisher, which is the fastest growing type of non-fiction publisher. Most of its authors invest in their own books, and have for-profit purposes for being published and distributed by a full-service publishing house, such as promoting themselves as thought-leaders, speakers, consultants, doctors, lawyers or investment advisors.

Astute entrepreneurs, executives and professionals often invest in status devices, tools, memberships, credentials, etc. but many businesses miss the opportunity to make being their customer –

and moving up their AP – a status purchase. Buying status is not necessarily (just) ego indulgence; it can be practical, and practically justified.

AP Example:

Let's apply this to a sample 'ordinary' business – a gourmet restaurant with extraordinary wine cellar.

We own a restaurant with an incredible wine cellar. Space available, anybody can make a reservation, come in, have dinner with or without wine, purchasing ala carte. But most of our customers will be led into our AP, and as many as possible moved up the AP level by level by level over time or "leap-frogged" to the top.

Level 1: VIP: bundles one evening a month, pre fix dinner for two with selected wine pairings, plus complimentary desserts, free dinner in member's birthday week, and the member newsletter, at a set price (automatically charged to the credit card on the first day of each month). Just for sample's sake, let's price this at $279.00 per month.

Level 2: GOLD VIP: bundles Level 1 with one invitation-only special tasting event 8 times a year, with visiting sommelier or chef, special wine tasting, and 4 guest passes for guests to join you for dinner once per 12 months. $379.00 per month.

Level 3: DIAMOND VIP – limited to 100 Members: bundles Level 2 with Select Wine Of The Month Club, providing you with a bottle of chosen wine every month, and guaranteed availability of reservations with 48 hours' request even for Valentine's Day and New Year's Eve. $547.00 per month.

Level 4: PLATINUM VIP – limited to 50 Members: bundles Level

3 with *access to* a place on the owner/sommelier escorted 4-day tour of northern California wine country and visits to 4 famous wineries + varied city excursions (additional per person fee required) OR access to a place at owner's summer beach-house weekend (no additional fee required) AND invitation to 4 different closed-door, special events during the year. $879.00 per month.

Levels #3 and #4 also include option of being featured in a profile or article in the monthly newsletter going to all the (affluent) "members," as well as spotlight interviews during an annual all-members' networking reception and event.

There, I think I've put all five of the AP "drivers" in.

Wasn't that hard, was it?

Of course, it does change *the nature of* the business – just like alchemy changes ordinary base metal to gold. It has to. What was just another upscale restaurant with a claim to fame of exceptional wine cellar, but, still, a wine cellar … to a prestige membership society featuring its AP. A *unique* business.

CHAPTER 6

PRICE LIBERATION

"I think you should be able to lease a dog."

- George Carlin

I believe I have had more impact on more business' profit improvement by price strategies than by anything else. This is possible in large part because **most business owners are Price Cowards!**

Because there is an entire book in my NO B.S. series – *NO B.S. PRICE STRATEGY*, I'm going to abbreviate comments here a lot and urge getting and reading that book. Here I'll focus just on Price Liberation. What does that mean? Most business owners' thinking about price occurs inside a very small prison cell, made of norms and standards and formulas. A prison break can be done, to great effect.

<u>What can just about any and every business do right now, today, to create some alchemy?</u> <u>Raise (some of) their prices. Simply or creatively.</u> Consider two businesses at the poor end of price: fast food restaurants and dollar stores. Dollar store chains have enjoyed great growth over the past decade, but more importantly they've grown profits, profit margins and sustainability by featuring $1.00, $4.00 - $5.00, and $9.00 – 10.00 pricing. There's even a chain called FIVE BELOW. The fast food chains introduced $1.00 Menus – but quickly figured out how to monkey with them, with $1.00, $3.00, $4.00 -

$5.00 items, and bundles of $1.00 items adding up to $3.00, $4.00 and $5.00. I differ with their tactics only over the round numbers.

Price and customer reaction to price is always about 5's and 10's. This is THE Principle to strategically and tactically apply.

You And I *Know* Better, But We Are Still Affected
(Because What We KNOW Matters Least)

When we see a really pricey item, say a luxury car, priced at $89,995.00, one part of our brain chuckles at the silliness of it. *Who are they kidding?* our brains say. It's ninety grand. Wowzer. But. Another part of our brain still reacts positively to the price coming in short of the 10, not quite the rounded up number with the zero at its end. We can't help ourselves. People *know* that they're being gamed with the $9.95 or $9.97 or $9.99, but they still *feel* a lot better about hearing it or seeing it than hearing or seeing $10.00. And I assure you with every fiber of my being and every ounce of my 47 years' experience, how they *feel* is much, much more important than what they know or think – before, during and after a purchase.

<u>All</u> pricing should either stop between a 4 and a 5 or if it is going to click over the 5, it might as well go to between the 8 and the 9 or the 9 and the 10. There is no reason to stop anywhere in between.

Personally, I have usually adhered to my own advice on this.

For many years, my base fee for a consulting day has been $18,800.00 for regular clients and $19,400.00 for a new client. I count this as getting an extra $800.00 and an extra $400.00 for these days. Because, in the consulting part of my business, I am a small, solo practitioner, this doesn't multiply as it would for a giant consulting enterprise or another type of professional practice with 6, 12, 24 doctors or lawyers or accountants under one roof. Still, in a typical year of late, I've been conducting about 10 new client days and about 30 regular client days, totaling $28,000.00 for a year in the extra money. Being paid for 1.5 days of no work. In 10 years, less taxes, plus interest, about a quarter of a million dollars. If that's trivial to you, congratulations. It's not trivial to me.

The information product I sold from the stage 30 to 40 times a year during my peak speaking years, *The Magnetic Marketing System®*, was priced for most of the times and in most of the situations at $397.00. Most years I sold over $1-million worth. The same product was also sold by direct-mail, placement in a number of catalogs, and by other means. I did some split-testing of different prices, dropping to $395.00 and going up to $399.00 and to $400.00, enough to persuade me that there was no difference in units sold, percentage of an audience buying, etc. from $397.00 down to $395.00, but there was slippage in quantity sold moving up from $397.00 just to $399.00, and a significant drop when trying the blatant round number of $400.00. Thus the $2.00 per unit between $395.00 and $397.00 was gravy. At 2,500 units a year for 11 years, that produced only an extra $55,000.00. I'll admit, arguably trivial, if any sum can really be trivial. Rockefeller carried handfuls of pennies in his pocket to toss to street urchins, but he reportedly never missed picking up a stray penny on the ground either. There is another test result with bigger ramifications regarding me and this product. Surprisingly, there was virtually no difference in units sold with the price dropped to $297.00. The extra hundred dollars times 27,500 units = $2.7-million, and that *isn't* trivial. Often, pricing is done by the assumption that a lower price buys disproportionately positive volume, but t'aint necessarily so. If there is going to be any volume, testing to find the right price could make a difference of millions of dollars over time.

In other words, you might bank relatively small gains by inching price up, but you can suffer large losses by under-pricing. Quoted elsewhere in this book, Buffett's #1 Rule of Investing is: *Don't LOSE Money*. It's the #1 Rule about Pricing, too.

Once I had a client selling an item by TV, in fairly large quantities, at a price of $29.95 after having split tested various prices from $19.95 all the way to $49.95. What he hadn't tested before my meddling was "2 payments of $19.95," which, although $10.00 higher, beat $29.95 by almost 2 to 1 in units of sale. Next, testing "2 payments of $24.95" also trumped the single $29.95," jacking the per unit price by $19.95. Multiplied by about 30,000 units sold, this produced an extra $598,500.00. In a very thin margin business, that makes a big difference. In his case it subsidized a costly cocaine habit, but that's beside the point. His under-pricing, entirely based on assumptions not split-testing* was robbing him of about a half-million dollars a year. (*Refer to Chapter #3)

The Grand Old Master of direct-response TV, Ron Popeil, had a secret method of establishing the stated shipping and handling charge for his various famous (infamous) products of the 1960's into the 1970's like Pocket Fisherman, Hair Spray In A Can, or the "set it and forget it!" countertop rotisserie oven: the S&H equaled the actual manufactured cost of the item plus the actual shipping cost! At the time, everybody else was charging just the actual shipping cost. Ron started the trend of making extra money by inflating the shipping. Today, in the era of free shipping on everything from diapers to furniture ushered in by Amazon (as a competition death blow), the Popeil Strategy no longer lives. It is still a great example, though, of the power of setting aside logic in pricing. This is an incredibly important idea: divorcing logic from price.

Ultimately, no pricing should ever be done casually or carelessly. Dimes add up to dollars. Dollars to tens of dollars. And so on. Nor should your thinking about price ever be boxed in by norms, formulas or fears.

Margin is even more important. Profit per product, per service and per customer is what loops back around to fuel (or dampen) growth, and to wealth, captive or extracted, for the business owner. There are big, public companies that enrich their founders and owners by stock valuation multiplying despite zero or little profit. This can't be denied. But it is somewhat like having a loose wheel or tire going bad and driving as fast as you possibly can before the inevitable wreck. As I was writing this, Elon Musk – who I consider a promoter who'd make P.T. Barnum blush – was up against some serious problems, from targeting and trying to maim short sellers of his company's stock by making unsubstantiated claims instantly scrutinized by the SEC. Regardless of how that turned out, Tesla is a prime example of corporate value detached from any semblance of present or future likely profit. Most business owners will never have the decadent luxury of such detachment. You are required to turn a profit. Therefore you should prioritize maximum possible profits. That will focus you on price.

Price stretching changes the cost to selling price math dramatically. An item with a hard cost of $10.00 sold for $20.00 has a 2X mark-up. 200%. A cost of goods of 50%. Somehow stretch the price to just $24.95 and you've raised the mark-up to 249%, a +25% boost. The cost stayed the same. If this does not reduce volume, you win big.

Price can also be a too easily accepted limitation to a business.

Price caps margin, up from all-in cost. One of the worst of the most common pricing practices is mark-up from cost by some industry standard formula. It makes cost govern, when **cost should be irrelevant in assessing value to the consumer by the consumer's own (or guided) perspective, i.e. willingness to pay** coupled with ability to pay. Whether you can price "x" at $10.00, $100.00 or $1,000.00 shouldn't have anything to do with its delivered cost of $5.00. Close your eyes to cost and work on maximum price possible to your customers without suppressing sales to a disadvantageous level, causing post-sale ill will that erases short-term profits or some other profoundly detrimental side effect. If you can achieve an "obscene" spread from cost to selling price, celebration, not guilt, is in order. Obscenity, after all, is in the eye of the beholder, and when I behold an extraordinary profit margin, I behold a magnificent work of art.

CHAPTER 7

The Power of Place Strategy

"Always drink upstream from the herd."

- **Texas Biz Bender**

In this chapter, I am going to give you keys to a much, much more lucrative and expandable business, by changing your thinking about where you get customers. The term for this is Place Strategy. It's a toss-up whether I have more impact on clients' businesses by Place Strategy or by Price Strategy, but this is definitely a powerful alchemic concept. The smallest and most mundane of businesses can be made gigantic and unique by it. It is alchemy because it has more to do with how you think, so as to knock down all imagined fences, than with anything else. It starts with a full and deep understanding of one simple fact:

MONEY IS MOBILE

Politician-idiots refuse to grasp the fact that Money is mobile.

It doesn't have roots like a tree. It has wings like a bird.

As I was writing this, a big hedge fund uprooted itself from Wall Street and moved to Nashville. Absurdly high taxes vs. low taxes; simple equation. More to follow. New Jersey, California are experiencing mass exodus of the rich and of companies. Texas and Florida beckon. The owner of a lot of West Virginia coal mines actually lives in Nevada, a no tax state. He can run businesses in one place but locate himself and all his money in another. Wowza! In 2018 Seattle proposed a new surcharge on large employers of $500.00 per employee per year, purportedly to aid the homeless. All that asinine idea promises is more homeless. But it was reversed within 2 weeks because Amazon and Starbucks threatened to move money and jobs elsewhere. *Finally*, a couple corporate titans with balls.

Even working folk figure this out. The really good waiter leaves the restaurant that forcibly pools tips and moves to one where he can leverage his superior skills, personality and attitude for higher, merit-based earnings. There was both driver and customer mutiny over Uber's egalitarian idea of equal pay for equal trip to any and all drivers; no tipping.

People know three things to be true:

1: Opportunity beats socialism*
2: Different people do the same job differently and deserve *unequal* pay
3: They can leave one place and move to another one offering better opportunity

This is under dangerous assault. We've had an entire 'lost generation,' lost to orchestrated ultra-Left indoctrination in universities, so that the economic philosophies of socialism and communism are viewed positively by a significant percentage of young people – instead of understood as oppressive scourges. This is a failure of factual education. Nothing less. However, for the moment, the majority still intelligently or intuitively reject it in favor of opportunity and personal ambition.

Money knows this as well. Money is *very* mobile. Don't try to cage your Money. It won't work. Instead, find the places in which it can happily produce the most.

This may mean geographic – but it might mean a myriad of other things too. Place is more than physical location.

A few years ago, I did some consulting and copywriting work for the State of Oklahoma, to strengthen its marketing aimed at companies located in high tax states, to relocate or expand in their business welcoming and friendly place. Larry Parman, then Secretary of Commerce, brought me in. In the year I was at work, I learned a lot about the seduction of money. The experience verified the principles I'd long known to be true, summarized in my book *No B.S. Wealth Attraction for Entrepreneurs (2nd Edition)*, and taught in depth in a trio of seminars available as audio programs at www.nobsinnercircle.com.

There were also discoveries. I discovered: companies, like people, shop. Big ones that know they will always grow have permanent, full-time next location or relocation shoppers. Others organize a project team to shop as needs develop. Either way, they *shop*. Like consumers, they rarely make a simple decision no matter how simple it seems. Like consumers, there are rational and logical, economic and financial, and emotional factors affecting a decision. It starts with what *isn't* wanted. Their current place(s) have been taking them for granted and stopped seducing them, so the temptation to look elsewhere grows. Foolishly, states compete by gifting financial incentives, notably featuring big tax breaks, to persuade new businesses to move in while never offering gifts and incentives to the companies already based there. Every state has a marketing operation like the one I worked with in Oklahoma, tasked with recruiting new businesses. NO state has a retention marketing operation tasked with keeping the ones they already have motivated to stay and grow and expand. There are hastily organized efforts to stop one from leaving once they've announced they're leaving, but this is almost always too late. The company's bags are packed and out on the stoop, a cab is waiting. A little late for seduction.

In short I saw the same stupidity in state governments and their commerce departments as I do in business: presumption that customers and their money will stay put, coupled with resentment at having to do anything to make them stay put.

The states have huge ad budgets for chasing new companies but <u>no</u> ad budgets to run a full page ad in *The Wall Street Journal* each month featuring their great companies and interesting start-ups and CEOs and entrepreneurs already in residence. They have big budgets and legislative willingness to reward a new company moving in, but <u>no</u> budget or legislative willingness to reward those hitting milestone anniversaries. Sure, the biggest corporate residents of a state have clout at the capitol – but none can get a deal for their next 5 years anywhere nearly as attractive and generous as their counterpart moving in for the first time. The thought process underlying this is that Money settles down and stays put. It doesn't.

Money is not only mobile, it's now global. There's this thing called the internet, that has shrunken the globe faster and more profoundly than the previous globe shrinking inventions – like the phone, air travel, FedEx. Once upon a time there was a neighborhood bakery. Now it ships its cupcakes all over *the world*. Your best customers may no longer be in a 5 mile or 50 mile radius or even in your home base country at all. Our own NO BS INNER CIRCLE has evolved from a membership almost entirely in North America to having nearly as many Members in overseas nations covering the alphabet A to Z as in our home land, and frankly, that by force of the market, not by wise and deliberate investment, focus and effort by its owners. A lot of U.S. businesses have the same situation: more accidental than purposed growth beyond our borders. It's a reality that should be listened to. By its movements, Money suggests Place Strategy.

In luxury goods, for example, the top markets are in Asia. Two automakers build 6-figure priced models exclusively for sale in Viet Nam. People my age still think of that place as rice paddies and Jane Fonda sitting on a tank. Out-dated ideas. The world has changed, and Nam has changed right along with it. The entrepreneur has to break himself free of old "visuals," old world views, provincialism, irrational and antiquated worry about the difficulty of cross-cultural marketing and international commerce. The highly effective golf instructor in residence at the country club in Cherry Hill, New Jersey has to scheme to give lessons by Skype or Zoom to golfers in Tokyo or in Saigon – for which he can charge a multiple of his hourly rate in New Jersey. <u>Every</u> business owner should engage in the same creative thinking.

You are <u>not</u> *actually* chained and constrained. The only thing confining you is your own mind-set. Today, even the smallest business can and probably should think globally or at least nationally, not locally. But "place strategy" and finding the places money can produce the most can be much more varied, creative and imaginative than just physical location.

MEDIA STRATEGY CAN BE ITS OWN LIBERATING PLACE STRATEGY

Media offers a wide array of Place Strategy opportunities.

As, essentially, an ad man, I am *a media creature*. Most business owners and corporate leaders are not, so they tend to default to the same media used by their peers and competitors, used in the same way as their competitors use it. By doing so, they fence their businesses in to small places. It also leaves them vulnerable to media sellers who sell the same media to all the competitors in a category, often by the least rational argument: you have to spend a lot of money here because your competitors do. But if all the other kids jumped off a high cliff into a shallow pond, your mother would ask, would you jump with them? Or have you a mind of your own to use?

I made a client a multi-millionaire by moving his Gold By The Inch home-based business opportunity centered around a portable, tabletop gold bracelet "store" from its magazine advertising to TV, with a 30-minute infomercial that aired for 9 consecutive years. Similarly, but on a much grander scale, my client Guthy-Renker deliberately kept its Pro-Activ® acne products 100% off store shelves, sold exclusively via TV infomercials, then other media – building a business sold for nearly $2-Billion. In both cases, Media Place Strategy --- where to be and where *not* to be --- was the chief cause of created value. To be clear, there are lots of manufacturers of gold chain, and gold chain is gold chain. But for nuance distinctions with little difference, acne glop is acne glop. You can find large varieties and quantities of both at any Target store. These two businesses differentiated by Place, not by product.

There are two ways there is alchemy in this. One, reducing presence in or staying out entirely of a media place everybody else in your category gathers. By this alone, you make money materialize. If you stop putting it in one place, it's available to move to a different place. If you lift it out of the bumper-to-bumper traffic jam full of who-can-honk-louder? competition and move it to a road much less traveled but with your potential customers housed along its path, you can multiply the impact of each dollar. A big percentage of your ad spend no longer needs go just to honking louder than the others, just to competing for attention. A bigger percentage can now move to making your case. Two, your money can now get your message to potential buyers BEFORE anyone else arrives, because you can *create* the interest and desire to buy instead of waiting for that to be present first.

Something as simple as a specialty medical practice can set aside its city boundaries and draw patients from the entire country by advertising in airline magazines and lifestyle magazines. It's done with hormone therapy, carpal tunnel syndrome, and anti-aging treatment. The doctor running full-page ads for anti-aging therapies in national travel, lifestyle and financial magazines is not waiting for somebody to be motivated by symptoms and illness or health dysfunction to then search for a provider. The doctor running this kind of ad campaign is circumventing search, getting ahead of need, thus disrupting normal consumer behavior, and creating interest and desire. He has moved his ad spend to a road much less traveled. He is getting to prospective patients first.

Think about what it *means* when a patient decides to travel from Minneapolis to Houston to see the nationally advertised doctor "wizard" instead of the doctors doing comparable work at the big name hospital or at a private practice at his home city of Minneapolis. VOLUNTARILY replacing 15 minutes' travel time with 5 hours. Mobile Money has chosen to move from where it is kept to where it will be spent, entirely due to the distant doctor *having a bigger idea* than the local ones, and to effective direct-response advertising and authority marketing in nationwide media instead of confining himself to local media and the local market ... a different Place Strategy altogether. This *guarantees* price/fee elasticity. This doctor *automatically* gets to charge *much* higher fees per hour, per procedure, per patient relationship, and to sell packaged multi-month "programs" instead of pay-as-you-go, pay-by-the-visit. By Place Strategy, he achieves the kind of Price Liberation discussed in Chapter #6.

In many ways, this is an old, classic success philosophy, practically applied. David Schwartz' famous bestselling book first published in 1959, *The Magic of Thinking BIG*, laid out and lays out the principle and the reality/opportunity. The principle is: think bigger to achieve bigger. The reality/opportunity is: almost everybody thinks small. If you condition yourself to think big, you gain enormous opportunity. This is such a universal dichotomy, there is even a scene in the film Butch Cassidy and the Sundance Kid about it. And a pre-President Trump quote: "If you're going to bother thinking at all, you might as well Think BIG."

There are two basic, foundational big ideas about marketing: one, show up like no one else. Two, better, show up like no one else AND SHOW UP ALONE.

PLACE YOURSELF WHERE YOU ARE NOT SUPPOSED TO BE AND WATCH WHAT HAPPENS!

Out Of Category media and sales venues offer as big and wide an array of opportunities as your imagination will allow.

As I mentioned, acne glop is *supposed to be* on the drug store shelves and in magazine ads, not half hour long TV infomercials. Gold chain is *supposed to be* at the jewelry counters in stores and at ecommerce sites, not packaged up as basis for a business opportunity, and then sold from pop-up stores at all sorts of "wrong" places ---- hotel lobbies, horse shows, swap meets and flea markets. Similarly, steaks and hamburgers are *supposed to be* sold at local butcher shops and supermarkets, not sold by TV, radio, print and online nationally, and shipped by FedEx to peoples' doors, as does Omaha Steaks and its competitors. You can go product category by product category and find such stand-out, trend-setting, enormously successful violators of where they are supposed to be.

A very-high-fee, "elite" matchmaking service, finding ideal mates and future trophy wives for affluent men advertises in --- *classic auto magazines.* As does Cengenics®, a version of the anti-aging medical practice I already spoke of. My client High Point University distributes its magnificent magazine for prospective students and their parents --- *on racks found only in private jet travel FBOs.* For several years, the aforementioned ProActiv® was advertised in local Yellow Pages books nationwide – *in the Dermatologist section.* These are prime, successful examples of Out Of Category Advertising.

Non-traditional distribution channels and places can be just as impactful. Cleveland Clinic has been shutting down its free-standing urgent care centers and replacing them with very "retail" Express Clinics located in high traffic shopping centers, next to popular stores like Hobby Lobby and Wal-Mart. Blue Apron hit a wall online and is experimenting with distribution at Costco.

Because I own racehorses, I attend racehorse auctions in Ohio. At every such auction, there are racehorse related vendors and exhibitors – and one "oddball," a pop-up jewelry store. I'm told it consistently out-performs mall stores in dollars and, more so, profits per square foot per hour of operation by a double digit multiple. Here's why: when I head out for the auction, my wife asks: "You aren't buying another horse, are you?" – to which the correct answer is: "No. Of course not. I'm just going to keep Ralph company." Ralph uses the very same script. As does every other married guy there. When we return home with a lead shank in one hand, attached to the halter of another horse, it is useful to have a new diamond tennis bracelet in the other. Since there is only one seller there, he gets 100% of this business at very elastic prices, no "free earrings with pendant" needed. This is a beautiful example of Out Of Category Place Strategy.

If you aren't always alert for and creative about "new/better place" and "more fertile fields" strategies, ready and willing to move, your Money can't move either. Whether it stays parked with you or, in disgust, leaves you altogether, the result is about the same. You lose.

This is of escalating importance in The Age of Amazon. I warn clients: if your business can be amazon-ed, and there's any money in it, it WILL be amazon-ed. It is the great commoditizer. Crusher of price, destroyer of profit. But it is entirely search driven. It is, in fact, a search engine. It can't (or won't) go set up its jewelry shops at a horse auction. Your survival may well depend on doing out of category things that Amazon and its cousins can't or won't do.

Personally, I have made a handful of critical and radical "moves" during my 46+ year career, the first of them very early, the most recent of them in 2018. None have been comfortable or convenient. But they have all been almost alchemic in results. Brave 'n bold and prescient movement attracts money. It's a magnetic force. In one of my big moves, I walked away from a place; a source of about $1-million a year in income and about $4.5-million a year in free advertising, without clarity about how to replace either the income or the advertising. Very quickly, other irons in the fire got white hot, new opportunities arrived, and both replacements occurred. I admit: thin line between recklessness and faith. Still, staying put was stultifying and on verge of going sour. If your Spidey sense tingles, you should do something about it. Like: *move*.

THE COSSMAN METHOD

E. Joseph Cossman was so famous at one time, over 2-million copies of his book *How I Made $1-Million In Mail-Order And You Can Too* were sold at a blazing fast clip. But the book was badly mis-titled, for, although Joe did use mail-order opportunities brilliantly, he was actually an early pioneer of what is now called "multi-channel distribution." Even more importantly, most of his more than 25 different million and multi-million dollar product successes brought to market, one after the other, over a 20 year span depended on one particular Method: Joe found "dead," failed or anemically selling products in one Place and creatively moved them to an entirely different Place. *He didn't invent anything*. He *moved* things.

I got to know Joe late in his life, when he was in semi-retirement; a wealthy man enjoying life in Palm Springs. We did a couple small but interesting projects together. In those few years, I learned every detail of what I've taken to calling The Cossman Method in his honor. It is elegantly simple and ingenious.

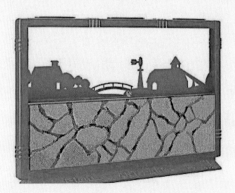

The greatest of his successes was a product called The Ant Farm. In a modified version, it lives on today, decades after its first success orchestrated by Joe Cossman. If you are near my age, you may well have had one of the originals in your bedroom, atop your dresser, to the distress of your mother. The Ant Farm was a thin plastic box, in which ants built their homes and tunnels in dirt, and it was all transparent from both sides, so you could watch them work and move dirt about and tunnel up and down and back again. It let you watch them underground! The original, small mail-order ad for the product duplicated here, at the end of these pages, tells its story. This is, incidentally, the kind of ad Joe often used to test the market appeal of a product before committing to its manufacture or, sometimes, even to inking an exclusive licensing contract for it. The direct to consumer advertising results were also used to persuade distributors, brick and mortar retailers and catalog houses to promote the product. (That same strategy has been the norm of TV infomercials and direct-response spots pushing products into retail for the past decade or so). It is significant that Joe often price-tested initially way below the intended, actual selling price, so as to cleanly test market appeal only. Joe also believed that if he couldn't write a compelling ad about a product, the product would be a flop in any distribution channel. In most cases, when his products went to the retail shelf, the box copy came from the ad copy.

The Ant Farm was a nothing-burger of a product when Joe found it. It was sold only by school supply companies, only to elementary school and high school biology and earth-sciences teachers for use in their classrooms. Therefore, the possible number of units to be sold was extremely constrained. It languished there for years. Joe leaped to the idea that every red-blooded boy would love to have the bugs and their invisible, underground habitat transformed to a secrets revealed, reality show. Why limit it to the school classroom? It reminded him of a fish aquarium, and kids wanted those. Surely bugs were more fascinating. So: a bug aquarium.

The Ant Farm was a huge success, sold by mail-order, in comic books, and in catalogs, but also in virtually every toy store and toy section of department stores nationwide. It garnered publicity on TV shows and in print media. All this far pre-dated media like Instagram, Facebook and YouTube, which could obviously have been used had they existed.

You may have products or services within your present business' portfolio, barely earning their keep, with enormous value waiting to be unleashed by relocating them ala The Ant Farm. And/or you may own a customer population or a distribution channel ideal as a moved-to place for someone else's unsuccessful product. Either way, The Cossman Method can work for you too.

ORIGINAL AD COPY:

FASCINATING "ANT HOUSE" – JUST $2.98

A house for ants? An ant house for kids? Yes, and mother and father have fun too! … watching the ants *after they go underground*, as well as above ground. See the busy worker ants digging tunnels, carrying their loads. Watch the feeder ants storing away supplies for the rest of the colony. The nursemaid ants caring for the ant babies. *An ant's entire world seen through the clear plastic walls of this fascinating house.* Only $2.98 including house, sand, sandbar and tabletop stand. From: Cossman Company, P.O. Box XXXX, Palm Springs, California 92263.

A Few Words About

SALES MANAGEMENT

A GIRL SCOUT IN SAN DIEGO SOLD A STAGGERING 300 BOXES OF COOKIES IN UNDER 5 HOURS, by placing herself and her sales table outside a marijuana dispensary. In this, there is a major lesson. If you have a good salesperson or sales team, you want to place them where they can be busy selling. You don't want them "prospecting" – that's like asking a racehorse to also pull the hay-baler in the field to make his own feed. There are a lot of ways to fail at sales management, and one of the most common is misuse of salespeople.

Sales Management done right is part of "ASSET MANAGEMENT," which determines how much or how little yield you get out of *everything you own* – from the real estate underneath your office to your production capacity to your lead flow and store traffic and lists to your sales team to your own skills and time. Given the same set of assets, one entrepreneur grows rich while another barely ekes out a disappointing living. Too many business owners are too often trying to add more (advertising, media, customers, salespeople) rather than focusing on doing more with the assets they already have. In most businesses, there is as much harvest going uncollected as there is being collected!

Most *incorrectly* think that sales management is managing the salespeople, but I assert it is as much or more about managing place/process so the salespeople are leveraged to their full potential, by having them in front of or on the phone with qualified prospects to sell to, *100%* of their time at work. That means *never* turning them loose to hunt by their own ideas and devices. If you were managing 20 Girl Scouts selling cookies and you turned them loose, what would most if not all do? Get Mom and Dad to help and take their order sheets to the workplaces for them, go to neighbors' doors, maybe set up a sales table in their front yard like a lemonade stand or (where I often see them stupidly placed) outside a supermarket. But given the item of information I started with (or a mix of common sense and creative thinking), you could put them in pairs and place them at sales stations outside every marijuana dispensary in your city – and in a single day sell more at each spot than the entire team would sell over weeks left to forage for themselves.

To paraphrase my friend Jay Abraham, be sure you are getting everything you can out of all you've got, before you take on 'more' and 'new' from which you won't get everything they can yield.

CHAPTER 8

THE ONLY POINTS ON THE SCOREBOARD

"There are <u>no</u> new fundamentals. <u>You've got to be suspicious</u>
of someone who says they've got *new* fundamentals.
That's like somebody inviting you to tour a factory where
they are manufacturing antiques. Watch your wallet."

- Jim Rohn

THERE IS THE NEW PROBLEM OF NONSENSICAL 'NEW METRICS'

*and there is the old problem of wanting to bank rewards
that can't be deposited at the bank.*

If either or both set up shop in your business, they'll turn it into
a fantasyland. A business is easily sucked into this. Everybody gets
trophies. This can get very expensive.

New metrics are fake news.

Charlatans promoting social media are the leaders in creating means
of fake success by their media and methods: likes, views, viral;
engagement, re-tweets, minutes of views, and on and on and on.
Any or all of these *may* be useful in dissecting a disappointing result
to find the places where repair or replacement is needed throughout
a sales process or in identifying what specific steps are leading to a

satisfactory result, so as to replicate that result with another product or service or process. But these metrics are <u>not</u> a result in and of themselves, anymore than buying a garden hose and taking it home to your garage is a watered, healthy lawn. Simply put, if it can't be put on the bank deposit slip, it's <u>*not a result*</u>. A horde of employees, consultants, vendors and others will constantly try persuading you otherwise. A pox on them all.

Lee Iacocca, the savior of Chrysler in the 1980s, personally told me of calling one executive after another into his office and challenging them to show by drawn diagram how what they did caused the sale of a car. Any who couldn't – 2 out of 3 – were summarily fired. This is the only rational approach to your investments in people or into media: can it prove it *causes* sales?

If not, *out.*

When they bring you just statistics but not sales results, they are bringing you fake news.

The only real news is sales.

The minute you re-focus everybody and everything on this single and only way points go on the scoreboard, you begin alchemy in your business, converting every activity, every investment, hell – every piece of paper into money. If you discipline yourself to insist on this one and only way of putting points on the scoreboard, you will be unpopular with many, judged stupid and unreasonable by many, but you *will* run up the score.

True story: a non-profit diverted over $1.5 Million from its traditional fundraising activities to online and social media, paying a team of three employees working with two outside agencies to "bring it into the 21ˢᵗ century," with a robust Facebook, Instagram, YouTube, etc. platform, a much enhanced website, and a lot of "content marketing."* After a year, the team gave the CEO and the Board a magnificent two-hour presentation with graphs and pie charts, proving their success entirely with new metrics – visits, views, engagement, viral. However, the number of new donors was static but the average dollar value had dropped by a stunning 30%, existing donors' contributions had fallen by 10%, and there was no evidence of any kind of a positive return on investment measurable in dollars. The team was positively orgasmic in describing all its successes. But none put any money points on the scoreboard. Imagine their shock when, before the day ended, they were disbanded, the entire "project" ended, the outside vendors terminated.

This is the hazard in permitting people to make up their own game and keep score as they see fit.

This is *not* a diatribe against online or social media. I am agnostic about media. It is a stand against nonsense. No media, no investment should get a pass. Every media and every investment should be held ruthlessly accountable *in dollars.*

At a recent NO BS INNER CIRCLE Member Conference we had, as a guest speaker, Alan Doan, who has built a truly amazing, multi-million dollar business in quilting, with his mother as the star of a robust and remarkably effective YouTube media platform. On the other hand, at about the same time, I featured a report in a NO B.S. newsletter on a much hyped and celebrated speaker with a giant social media following and YouTube success as claims to fame, but with shockingly little to show from it all, financially. Given those two examples, what are we to make of YouTube? The same thing we are to make of any and every media: it must be tested and judged situation by situation, factually, financially. There is no such thing as universally "good" or "bad" media investments. There are situationally profitable and unprofitable investments in media.

TRUTH IS NOT SUBJECTIVE.

Entirely by accident, I recently heard a song, I think you'd classify it as country-rock, I think titled "Match Made In Heaven." Its main lyric is: *"You've got lips that taste like honey and I've got big money."*

Did you cringe?
#InconvenientTruths

It made me think about how many inconvenient, uncomfortable, usually denied truths there are about what *really* makes the world go 'round, how the world *really* works, how the sausage is *actually* made at the hog farm 'n factory, what people *really* think, believe and feel privately that governs their actions. A lot of things are remarked on as "inexplicable" when, in fact, there are simple and straightforward explanations – ones people prefer pretending don't exist. Like hard-wired human nature. Like gender differences. Like digital *addiction*. Like 90% of people having malleable, situational (not absolute) ethics. And so on.

In the late 1930s into the 40s, the much-revered Napoleon Hill wrote about a collection of 'laws of success,' principles accepted as admirable by a consensus majority of the population, certainly by a majority of the market for success literature within that population. He largely held up a magnifying mirror to what was already believed in: persistence, organized effort, "the golden rule," etc. But his most ignored advocacy was for ACCURATE Thinking. I think, talk, write about it a lot, and push clients, Titanium Members and others about it a lot. In the same way that deep fascination with one's work and preference for it over most other activities most of the time is labeled by the majority who hate their work as "workaholism," accurate thinking is demon-labeled as "cynicism." So, those of us who engage in it often keep it to ourselves. Never, for example, mentioning the lyric I did above.

In selling to especially affluent/high value customers, we can never work hard enough at accurate thinking about them, accurate understanding of them. Buffett says he bought NetJets because he wanted to stop flying commercial but felt guilty and uncomfortable about the "flashy" rich man's indulgence of flying around by obscenely expensive private jets. I believe him. I don't share his discomfort about it, but I do get it. And a lot, if not most affluent consumers are held back from buying and owning, especially visibly owning different products or services because of emotional discomfort. Not factoring this in, and making it "okay" to own what you sell is a mistake. That's just one example. Accurate understanding of a 'type of' person is complex.

In captaining a company, accurate thinking is extremely difficult, because you are encircled by people who, for their own agendas or merely by ignorance, are all *inaccurate thinkers*, constantly bringing you fake news – like "new metrics," as example. In this captain's role, accurate thinking against all tides is vital. It all starts with *not* characterizing it negatively in any way – as cynical, "negative," narrow-minded, "old school," old-fashioned, unreasonable. It has a perfectly suitable name: accurate. That one name is sufficient, all others superfluous. It's also useful to keep in mind that facts do <u>not</u> foreclose creativity, any more than the truth of the above lyric --- that humans are transactional creatures engaged in pros-and-cons, quid pro quo, barter of one kind of benefit for another --- precludes genuine affection or even romance. Ayn Rand's Objectivism, an acknowledgement and pursuit of self-interest, does not *prohibit* your fulfilling others' self-interests. Often, the latter is the only way of achieving the former. It actually works better with honesty about chief motivation, at least to oneself.

CHAPTER 9

END THE DE-VALUATION
OF YOUR OWN DOLLARS

"Money often speaks to me. Its vocabulary seems limited, though.
Mostly to: 'goodbye, sucker.'"

- Bob Orben

The worst and most financially inefficient approach
to advertising and marketing is ***democratized spend***.

Let me explain *most carefully*, for this is a crippling mistake so
commonly and consistently made that, should you stop, you'll be
the lone strong-man walking upright with big strides, surrounded by
hunched over cripples shuffling along.

Most businesses indiscriminately distribute their ad and marketing
dollars, like spraying water from a backyard sprinkler evenly, all over
the lawn.

A budget is established, a list of media picked; budget divided by media; presto! Spend! This is how Money is disrespected. It's how media and advertising returning very poor ROI gets equality with media and advertising returning high ROI.

Many silly reasons contribute to this, notably including the peer and competitor pressure to be seen somewhere and the ego frustration with not being seen there. **But the biggest reason is, bluntly, simple ignorance about differential ROI.**

If you won't take the time and trouble to learn, understand and manage ROAS (Return On Ad Spend) in your business, you shouldn't be allowed to advertise at all. Friends don't let friends drive drunk.

To illustrate this in a powerful way, I asked my friend and a client, Timothy Seward, Founder and CEO of ROI REVOLUTION to step in and contribute to this chapter. His company manages hundreds of millions of dollars of ad spend on Google, Amazon and other platforms for major "name" companies – doing for them what they won't do for themselves: UN - democratized spending. Often with dramatic results.

For 16 years, his team of 170+ analysts, data crunchers, media buyers and account managers have helped more than 290 brands, retailers and ecommerce merchants in 7 countries create bigger and faster growth with better profits, lowering costs by their deep, deep detective work and constant vigilance along with their proprietary technology. This unmatched experience from work with clients like Kenneth Cole, Perry Ellis, Time-Life, Plow & Hearth and Hammacher Schlemmer informs what you are about to read.

If you advertise and use pay per click with online media, his disclosures here have specific relevance. But even if you don't, it is a demonstration of alchemy.

"MONEYBALL" IN BUSINESS

by Timothy Seward

One thing you quickly learn about Google, after spending time interacting with their team, is their data-driven approach to almost *everything.* From the food served in its cafeterias to the placement and type of ads on its main search page, *data drives nearly all decisions.*

Google had just 800 employees when it moved into their Mountain View, CA campus headquarters, nicknamed the Googleplex, in 2004, and by the following year they already employed a few thousand people. My first moment on Google's campus came in July 2005, following an invitation by one of Google's product managers, and since then I have been on Google's main campus about a dozen times – interacting with their engineers, their agency sales teams and even briefly with former Chairman Eric Schmidt (and a couple close encounters with co-founders Sergey Brin and Larry Page).

Google's stock price recently (July, 2018) broke the $1,200/share barrier. Of course the most important thing to understand about the company is that it makes nearly 90% of its revenue from online ads.

Brands are willing to pay Google so much each month because the company owns the most visited website and search engine in the world (youtube.com is #2 and facebook.com is #3 according to Alexa's "Top Sites" report) and it knows a lot about its users, enabling it to show tailored ads to the right people at the right time.

Of course there are many reasons driving Google's dominance, but likely it's fueled by its relentless focus on users and its obsession with using data to drive nearly all of their decisions.

In 2003, author Michael Lewis published *Moneyball*, a book about the Oakland A's baseball team and its general manager Billy Beane. The movie, starring Brad Pitt, was released in 2011. Its focus is the team's <u>analytical, evidence-based approach</u> to assembling a competitive baseball team, despite Oakland's disadvantaged revenue situation compared to richer clubs (such as the NY Yankees). This approach brought the A's to the playoffs in 2002 and 2003.

Compared to the (then) *uber* successful Yahoo.com, in the first few years of Google's birth you could say that Google was in a disadvantaged situation just like the Oakland A's. It's my belief, based on personal observation and a variety of published accounts, that Google used an analytical, evidence-based approach to literally everything that eventually contributed to Google having the winning advantage over Yahoo.

What About Your Company?

In the next 12 pages, we're going to talk about Google, Google Shopping and Amazon and remarkable case histories of losses incurred by unsophisticated ad spend, and coming opportunities for growth --- much of it you feel you have a handle on. I get that. But the executives of all the companies we work with will tell you the same thing I'm telling you:

Force yourself to dig in. Be infinitely better informed than most of your direct competitors and your entire peer community.

If your company were being "embezzled" and losing tens to hundreds of thousand dollars – would you want to be told about it? Be the one to stop it – or the person horse-whipped for it when others discovered it? (Believe me, *this* is a conversation you want to take the lead on.)

That's exactly what these kinds of losses do. Ad over-spend, misdirected ad spend, missed availability of the highest possible ROAS (Return On Ad Spend) does not stop with the dollars lost within. It does further harm – a big multiple, in terms of "lost opportunity cost."

You may have heard Kevin O'Leary on TV's Shark Tank talk about his investment dollars as soldiers sent out to battle, plunder and bring back treasure. Every over-spend, misaimed spend, missed % in ROAS depletes your army and gives you fewer remaining soldiers. A dollar lost is a dollar that can't be reinvested to multiply.

If an 8:1 ROAS is available, every dollar surrendered to the kinds of losses we stop for clients is really $8.00 lost. $10,000.00 unnecessarily lost is actually $80,000.00. $100,000.00 is nearly $1-Million. And that is a lot of loss.

Once upon a time, not that long ago, it was relatively easy to make money with Google fueling the growth of your business – so, bluntly, you could be SLOPPY and get away with it.

Many business owners and executives turned blind eyes and deaf ears to whatever their marketing managers were doing with digital ad spend, and everything came out okay in the wash. Many marketing teams inside companies got very spoiled by this. But all that is now an unaffordable luxury. A path to ruin.

So, let's get into some case history stories ...

Last fall we were beginning to see less year-over-year growth for one of our most loyal clients. As a direct to consumer retailer in a low-price point market, they had a strict $10.00 CPA (advertising cost per order) upper limit. The $10.00 limit was holding us back from growth, because we could see much higher impression share available on Google than they were getting due to simply being "outbid" by some of their competitors.

Revenue was being reported in Google Analytics, but we could see the order size variance and asked our client "point person" if they'd be willing to incorporate a technology we developed called COGS (Cost of Goods Sold) that would give us (in Google Analytics) *true gross profit tracking*.

By tracking actual gross *profit* (rather than just gross revenue) we were able to bid higher on keywords driving higher priced/ profit products and lower on keywords, which drove lower priced/ profit products. It ended up resulting in a wonderful change! After four years of nearly flat growth, this retailer's results started to take off in the month we implemented the changes (August). By November, we hit their highest monthly transactions and revenue to date:

30% increase in overall transactions

29% increase in revenue

Adspend at $10.34 CPA

The More You Know ...

Many decades ago, then one of the three richest men in the world, Aristotle Onassis, proclaimed THE secret to his success was simply knowing things others did *not* know.

One of the things we often do – with our proprietary GATE technology – is create a second, parallel universe Google Analytics profile that takes a different and wider view of your conversion funnel. This gives you insight into (the secret about) how prospective clients *first* learn about your company.

The standard Google Analytics conversion tracking is a last touch attribution model. It reports on the click made just prior to purchase. It doesn't accurately measure first touch; how people FIRST became aware of you and your brand.

For example, people who do a generic search click on a non-branded, generic keyword, but two days later return to your site via your branded ad. By not understanding their movement from the very start, you can make COSTLY mistakes – like giving your branded ads too much credit or by spending on unprofitable keywords or by not spending on viable and important ones.

When we set up and monitor this additional, alternative analytics profile in Google Analytics, we are able to detect which, if any, of these non-branded keywords are, in fact, driving sales further into your funnel. This is a much more sophisticated approach than your competitors are using, so there can be significant competitive advantage. We can actually know, not guess or hope, which unbranded keywords are profitable, producing customers.

Home Goods Retailer Sees Growth
for Three Consecutive Years

In 2014, an industry-leading home goods retailer and ROI Revolution client was experiencing quick growth and profits from customers purchasing online. Through traditional media forms, they found monumental success from branded advertising and were looking to expand their market through untapped and underutilized digital advertising channels.

Online behavior trends for 2015 indicated that, during a sale, customers were taking less time to do research and were making more impulsive purchases. The opportunity was there to create a low-friction experience on their website to convert customers through non-branded search queries. With this in mind, they turned to ROI Revolution to optimize their non-branded campaigns and accelerate their digital growth.

At the time, the home goods retailer's account was not set up to measure non-branded search campaigns (including those fueled by Google Shopping) holistically in the overall paid search program. Without a first-touch attribution tracking profile, it was difficult to determine how new customers learned of the company; whether through SEO, PPC, inbound marketing, or other channels.

Without proper and accurate tracking, the ad spend on non-branded keywords was not being considered as essential to bringing in online sales and revenue. It became critical to measure data on initial keywords and search queries to understand a broader picture of the buyer experience and identify opportunities to acquire new customers.

Using our GATE technology, we built and applied a custom attribution model to filter Google Analytics tracking code. This allowed data to be tracked on first-touch attribution for keywords and converted sales in addition to the default last-touch attribution model.

In collaboration with the home goods retailer and based on a more holistic attribution model, non-branded campaigns were launched centering on buyer personas and customer intent. Our analysts coupled this with targeted ad copy that channeled traffic to relevant landing pages giving the customer exactly what they were searching for on Google. Having this relevant experience doubled conversion rates and profitability due to the high relevancy to the customer.

As the non-branded campaign momentum grew, the custom first-touch attribution model revealed that, on average, the home goods retailer had a 35% shift of sales attributed to broad, top-of-funnel keywords from branded keywords. This data gave confidence to continue investing in the non-branded strategy with an increased budget. With more budget and a targeted, non-branded experience, ads reached a wider audience but still maintained relevancy and a high return on ad spend (ROAS).

Prior to ROI Revolution's involvement in 2014, online transactions via paid search were low and static. In 2015, those numbers skyrocketed. In every successive month from January to November, transactions rapidly increased. The home goods retailer ended the year with more than 20x non-branded transactions year over year (YOY).

Amazon Domination Will Continue: Where Are You?

Amazon is an existential, expanding threat. At the same time, Amazon is a grand frontier of epic opportunities. In fact, it may be the last, best expansion opportunity for brand, retail and e-commerce companies yet.

Why? It's widely expected that Amazon will drive 80% of the ecommerce growth in the United States over the next five years. 80%.

And while US ecommerce currently accounts for just 12% of consumer retail spend, that number will likely double over the next five to ten years.

Where are YOU – with this "Gold Rush"? Or "Danger"?

I'll be blunt. I don't know of any other "team" available for hire, who understands marketing on Amazon as thoroughly as my team. None. Anywhere. At any price.

Incredibly, most agencies handling search, online and social media don't even have a dedicated Amazon team in place – even though 49% of all US product searches begin at Amazon, by-passing Google, Bing, Facebook, etc. Let me tell you what that means:

Once upon a time, a town, Kingman, Arizona flourished, because you had to drive through it, going from Phoenix to Las Vegas and back again. If you had a restaurant, gas station, convenience store or other shop on its main drag, you couldn't help but make a lot of money. Even if you had a local tavern downtown, money poured in. Motels were full with people stopping for the night. Then a freeway by-pass was built. You can zip right around Kingman as if it wasn't there.

That's what Amazon is to a fast growing number of shoppers and information seekers: the expressway by-pass around Google et al. Zoom, zoom.

IF your company has an inexpertly strategized and poorly optimized – or non-existent – Amazon strategy, you could lose control of your products and pricing to grey marketers and counterfeiters.

IF you do not know precisely how to "LOCK IN" highest possible organic rankings at Amazon – that continue whether you are buying paid ads a lot, a little or not at all - you will be pushed aside, marginalized, and even destroyed, if the percentage of online search owned by Amazon climbs from 49% to 54% to 63% to 71%.

IF your company is not managing day-to-day changes, catalog listing issues, data feed 'gotchas' that occur for virtually every brand or merchant at Amazon, your order flow could collapse to a trickle without warning.

IF you are not "strategic planning" *ahead of* the evolution of Amazon and Amazon Marketplace, you could miss out on absolutely amazing opportunities for growth of revenue and brand status and power – for, like the Gold Rush, there is a limit to the land and productive mines, there is a "pecking order".

To know these things, you need an independent, objective, outside Amazon Advertising Audit.

Frankly, brand, retail and ecommerce companies' Amazon houses are on fire. They are already late and being left behind. Structural mistakes, lack of specific and insider knowledge, and negligence is already revealing itself. With our 260+ clients, we have worked over-time and then some to prevent the fires, get ahead of the dangers, and position for maximum profits going forward.

View Amazon as a Marketing Platform

Because Amazon captures more product search volume than any other online alternative in the US, you'd be crazy not to stand up and shout your name when consumers are looking for products in your category. Even if consumers are buying products elsewhere, they're either discovering them or 'drilling down' while researching, making it a key marketing platform.

Got a new product launch? Launch it on Amazon FIRST, and accelerate (or test) the sale of your new products without big budget national ad campaigns involving television and/or radio.

You may have worked in Google AdWords, so you know that your level of ad spend has no real impact on organic search rankings. Regardless of what you advertise, how you advertise or how much money you pour into advertising on Google, a tide that lifts your SEO ranking never occurs. Some conspiracy theorists and charlatans claim otherwise, but our experience managing $300-million dollars a year of paid advertising AND managing organic search for dozens of companies says: No. Sorry. One has nothing to do with the other.

If your own team or some other agency has been telling you the fairy tale that these things link, to push you into more spending – well, beware!

With Amazon, however, the fairy tale comes true.

Your amount of ad spend in 'Sponsored Products' at Amazon *directly impacts* your organic rankings and traffic flow, which in turn means you'll win the Buy Box War more and more and more often. Your ad spend earns you organic search benefits. You might argue Google as an egalitarian democracy and Amazon as a meritocracy. Amazon's "Theory Of Business" is that the more you spend on advertising on Amazon, the more customers you get, the more orders that occur, the more reviews you garner, the more authoritative and reliable your company is and the better your products are. Therefore, they direct the most traffic to the "best" companies on their platform, and they also starve the "worst" companies, hoping they'll go away. At the same time they are letting you win the Buy Box, they are sticking daggers into your competitors for you.

Consider the closed "power" loop: by being very, very wise abut Amazon and very, very sales-efficient with Amazon you can afford to spend more on advertising at Amazon. This in turn gets you more and more extra, FREE advertising at Amazon (organic search), pulled from generic search terms thus (most likely) new, virgin customers for you. This in turn denies your competitors' access to those customers and revenue. This in turn lets you spend more on advertising at Amazon. This in turn gets you more and more extra, FREE advertising at Amazon (organic search), pulled from generic search terms thus (most likely) new, virgin customers for you. This in turn denies your competitors' access to those customers and revenue. Each time you win the Buy Box, this entire loop has occurred. Isn't that fun?

You can create long-term value on Amazon for your products by building a deliberate link between keywords and keyword-optimized product pages that show off the best images and features of your product and continue to provide highly ranked organic search results in conjunction with your Amazon paid advertising campaigns. To improve Amazon conversion, improve content completeness and content quality.

Scale Profits With Amazon Advertising

Polk Audio was looking for an agency to help scale revenue and profits to surpass their Amazon sales goal. Polk was interested in new ideas and strategies to test in their Amazon Advertising account to gain non-branded traffic and conversions in their very competitive product categories.

Polk found it challenging to find time to manage their account consistently and implement best practices. They were unsure if and where their investment in Amazon advertising was actually driving business so they were unclear where to invest more and where to trim back. Also, they wanted assurance that their advertising dollars were being used as effectively as possible to drive results at a low ACoS (Advertising Cost of Sale) while maintaining a strong brand presence against competitors who were trying to steal their brand traffic (by advertising against Polk

Audio keywords and product pages).

Our Amazon ad team worked closely with Polk to understand what products to push and pull back in specific product categories. Additionally, more hands-on attention on the account allowed for more bid management control and a decision was made to increase spend on best selling products to win clicks on non-branded searches and defend traffic on branded searches (by placing ads in such a way as to lock out Polk's competitors).

Next, our team setup product display ads to help upsell with lower priced Polk items/products as add-ons to a main product. For example, Polk offers varying tiers of their popular sound bars that are as much as $50.00 more (upsell) or smaller speakers that could complement the initial shopper's product purchase selection.

After months of scaling revenue and profit by increased investment in their account, during Q4 2017, overall branded orders increased 7x over Q4 2016 at the same ACoS (which is their goal ACoS).

If you are a well-known brand owner or a reseller (with exclusivity on the products you sell on Amazon) with gross Amazon revenue of at least $50,000/month contact my company for an Amazon advertising audit and opportunity review.

————

TIMOTHY SEWARD
Founder and CEO

Timothy leads ROI Revolution in its mission to be the best in the world at managing measurable, results-driven digital advertising for retailers, brands, and ecommerce merchants. Timothy founded the agency in June of 2002. With his extensive marketing and retail background, he has spoken at industry ecommerce and retail events including IRCE, is a frequent guest lecturer at North Carolina State University's College of Management and has contributed to key industry publications including Internet Retailer.

Timothy is a Summa Cum Laude graduate of Florida Gulf Coast University with a bachelor's degree in Computer Science.

CHAPTER 10

Looking For Answers In All The Wrong Places
(Asking Alchemy Of Lettuce 'n Kale)

"We can't solve problems by using the same kind of thinking we used when we created them."

- Albert Einstein

THE CLIENT HAS A TALE OF WOE.

They have conquered a lead generation effort, getting an astounding 38% response to a free information offer to cold, rented mailing lists, from a wonderfully inexpensive single page letter. But the conversion to their $1,000.00 sale from these leads comes in at only 2.4%, which is not enough to profit, after all the costs of follow-up on the leads. Wave the white flag?

Not on your life.

They hoped I might somehow fix the conversion sequence, write better copy for those materials. To their disappointment, this is the last thing I wanted to do. To make this work, they needed a 4% conversion rate. Nearly double. And all the sales material had been written by two top copywriters. I could improve it, but with nominal boost, not *double*.

This highlights how people look for answers in all the wrong places.

If there ever was alchemy, it was done with combining of base metals and chemicals – and sorcery. Not lettuce and kale.

It was possible, even likely, that the 38% was too good. That copy might be made more exclusionary, to discourage those not seriously interested and financially capable of buying. If you drop the 38% by 5, 10, even 20 points, all the costs of follow-up drop proportionately. Or there might be a way to speed up the conversions, also reducing follow-up costs. But the best answer is none of the above. It is more complicated.

They have a campaign that works. Its only problem is their product's selling price. To leave the 38% at 38% and leave the 2.4% at 2.4%, they need a $1,400.00 selling price instead of a $1,000.00 selling price. Or, by some means, $400.00 more from each buyer or that by average – for example $800.00 more from some buyers. *This* is the place to work. If we can do some Price Strategy and other Financial Re-Engineering, we can make their successful lead generation campaign pay.

Doing Something We'd Rather Not Do, To Get A Result We Very Much Want Has A Name: Maturity

I spent the next two hours laying out *five different ways* to raise the average per customer by at least $400.00, thus allowing the successful campaign to be run at max speed to the entire available list population. Three of the five had to do with Price Strategy, the other two with drop-down offers shown only to those refusing to purchase the original product. A

6th could be selling of the unconverted leads to another, non-competing marketer. There would be no *one* answer. Certainly not from better sales copy. There would be no *simple* answer.

The client was <u>not</u> a dummy. This situation occurred within a $70-million business built from scratch, around very clever marketing concepts and innovative, proprietary products. Still, the smart client had a dumb reaction. He did his best to conceal his disappointment but I have been doing this work for 46 years with thousands of clients and I can sense unexpressed frustration with me like Yogi The Bear can sense a jelly doughnut in a picnic basket a mile away. He had come fully prepared to invest 6-figures in having me write new copy for this campaign and his other main pieces. But he was not willing to invest the same fee in having me work out all the details of the five suggested components of the needed bridge over the money gap stopping his use of the campaign. I watched he and his team depart, both of us empty-handed. The adjective for my watching their departure is: *wistfully*.

The root cause of missed opportunities, lost revenue and profits, weaknesses in businesses and outright failures is: looking for a simple solution to a complex problem or opportunity. Nothing is more self-sabotaging. The desire for it is understandable. Maybe even hard-wired. It took a long time in human evolution to set aside the simple solution to hunger --- spear hunting and killing a beast and eating it, to replace this with the much more complicated solutions of farming, ranching, food refrigeration, and Grubhub.

People often come to me in heat for a simple solution. They rarely get it. No important success is ever simple, even when it is made to look and seem that way. **Sustainable wealth-making involves embraced complexity**. If you will examine every significant business or individual success with this in mind, it will leap out to you as obvious as Holmes' trout in a bowl of milk. And you need look no further than Amazon. It began, struggled and would have died as a simple online bookstore. It is immensely valuable and powerful today as an *extremely* complicated, multi-faceted, multiple income streams, B2C and B2B enterprise. It has even embraced the very thing it once sought to kill: brick and mortar retail.

If you create a winning strategy, marketing campaign, product, etc. made impractical by one problem, my advice is (1) don't give up on it too easily – things like lead generation mailings pulling 38% response are not plentiful; and (2) don't look for a single, simple solution to the one problem standing in the way of exploiting the asset. (3) If profitability is the only problem, fix the math, not the marketing. The best marketing, the best sales copy, the best of everything won't overcome bad math.

Good Math, Bad Math.
Rich Entrepreneur, Poor Entrepreneur

I am going to convene a math class – and I know you would much prefer art class or recess. This is a class in what I call Money Math. You could call it Alchemy.

For starters, I am going to reveal an inside secret of most business fortunes and virtually all direct marketing fortunes: he who can spend the most money to acquire customers wins. Not he who has the best product in its category. Not he who delivers the best service. Not he who is purest of heart. Not he who has the best advertising. He who can spend the most money to acquire customers. This makes your MAC/CA – Maximum Allowable Cost for Customer Acquisition

THE, THE, THE MOST IMPORTANT NUMBER of all numbers in your business. Every inch you can expand it puts you miles ahead of your competition.

Next, another unsung secret: getting to the best possible MAC/CA is complicated. It will involve creating a spider web of monetization methods and opportunities surrounding the acquired customer. It will involve horizontal and vertical monetization. And monetization by internal and external means.

As the end of this chapter, you will find a condensed version of my FOUND MONEY MAP. This is the Map that I use to explore every advertising and marketing related financial nook 'n cranny of a client's company, in search of money to fuel exploitation of the above disclosed secret. I have never published this Map before, and have only provided it to private clients and attendees at very expensive seminars. Not all of it will immediately make sense to you; a little patience and persistence is worthwhile. You may not know all the terminology, if unfamiliar with direct marketing. There are a few "inside baseball" references that only my serious followers would know. Still, I've provided this document "as is" and if you wind up with significant questions about it, I invite your queries by fax: 602-269-3113.

The Map has 45 probative questions and a 2-page chart. I have added a brief glossary of terms. It is meant to be something of *a workshop* – not something to read and move on from.

As summary, the principle behind all the strategies and tactics, behind maximum monetization of a customer: You should be chronically, perpetually unsatisfied with anything less.

NEXT.

NEXT is the single ***most valuable word*** in customer monetization.

If you will make it your most important word, your most often and insistently asked question, you will find and create real alchemy inside your existent customer population and money flow. The question is: now that they have done this, what is Next?

There should **_never_** be an end to *any* road you place a customer on. Always a next, Next. Back door to front door, exit ramp to (choice of) next on ramp(s), extension(s), upward mobility and ascension, etc., etc., and etc. – all applied NEXT.

Rigorously inspect your business for roads with dead-ends.

DAN S. KENNEDY'S
FOUND MONEY MAP

"If the core of every thought you have, when you wake up in the morning and go to sleep at night is: how can I make more money? – you will be shocked at how much more money you will make."

- Gene Simmons (KISS)

SAMPLE QUESTIONS FOR FOUND MONEY MAP

INTERNAL

PRICE

1. Where is the business **priced *below value*** (giving into other influencing factors)?
2. Is there a simple, broad price increase warranted and doable?
3. Is there opportunity for tiered pricing?
4. **SEGMENTING:** different prices to *different buyer populations* for same product?
5. Promotional Pricing – better front-end offer?
6. How have price decisions been made (in the first place)?

    (Formula; Industry Norm; Competition; Guesswork; Fear)

SELLING

Analyze the 'selling event' …

7. **WHO** is doing the selling … to WHO? (Match?)
8. **WHERE** is the selling taking place?

    (egs: space designed for it or borrowed corner of office used for other purposes)
9. **CHOREOGRAPHY:** what occurs in what order?
10. **CHOREOGRAPHY:** script/action for everybody
11. **WHEN** does the selling occur? (Organized or random)
12. *TIME INVESTED BY PROSPECT*
13. **DEMONSTRATION?**
14. **FIRE & HIRE:** l wrong people, "dead" people doing the selling.
    ●NEVER One. ● "3 Strikes And You're Out"
15. **PROSPECT PREP:** what goes on leading up to selling? IMMEDI-ATELY PRECEDING selling?

LOSS PREVENTION

16. Is company managing and monetizing *just buyers* or leads?

17. "Appointment, No Sale"?

18. Are there *"disaffection* alarm bells" in place?

19. Actual theft and embezzlement controls?

20. Financial "standards"?

21. Predictive Indicators (or just Trailing Reports)?

22. Cyber-security?

EXTERNAL

GROWTH

23. For what product/service of the business is there an (obvious) higher value customer (not being deliberately targeted)?

24. Is there an asset being poorly used or poorly leveraged?

    (egs.: top salesperson doing things other than selling. Cache client; claim to fame client/ case history not used for peer-target marketing. Significant Story not being told.)

25. Is there a (possible) Demonstration(s) not being used? – *or not being done theatrically* and dramatically?

(Houdini: straight-jacket escape on stage vs. hanging upside down from a crane 100-feet in the air. Sam Pitts infomercial: wheelbarrows of mail, crew of workers opening envelopes, removing checks, tallying money.)

26. Is there a failure to List Segment & Message Match?

27. Is *differential* customer value tracked? Used?

28. What are the (current? Chronic?) top 3 roadblocks to growth? – and who is working on removing them?

29. What is the scheme to allow for *highest* possible customer acquisition costs?

30. **STRAIGHT LINES:** What is *"THE NATURAL NEXT"*? (EXTEND each product and each service.)

31. **STRAIGHT LINES:** What new need/problem does success with the business' products or solutions create?

32. **PYRAMID:** What can be assembled to create higher/deluxe levels of the already successful product or service? (One aimed at 20% of customers; another at 5%.)(egs.: coach, first class, clubs, now new "super elite" terminal at LAX - $7,500 a yr + $2,800+ per use.)

33. **PYRAMID:** Can there be horizontal movement from one pyramid to a 2ⁿᵈ, same customer held in both? (egs.: KIC/IMA. Country Club>Travel Club.)

34. **SPIDER WEB:** What attaches to what you do?
(egs.: I write copy to which graphic production attaches, mailing list procurement attaches, video production attaches, etc. When I wrote copy for Miracle Ear, procurement of celebrity attached, mystery shopping of inbound calls attached.)

35. 35): **SPIDER WEB:** How many possible sources of money can be connected to a single "business unit"? … then again to each of those?

EXPANSION /// DIVERSIFICATION
OUTSIDE-BUSINESS MONEY

36. Are there **ignored Distribution Channels?** (Disney's "inappropriate" use of Spencer Gifts.)

37. Is there an unexploited Re-Purposing/Place Change opportunity? (E. Joseph Cossman's #1 Strategy.)

38. Is there outside-biz money available INSIDE something being done/ that has to be done anyway? (egs. Selling "real estate" to others in my books.)

39. Where are SYNERGY OPPORTUNITIES?

40. What are the OPC opportunities?

41. What SUBSIDIES are possible?

42. **HORIZONTAL = FOLLOW <u>THEIR</u> MONEY** (What else are THEY buying?)

43. **VERTICAL = FOLLOW <u>YOUR</u> MONEY** (What are you buying at

retail that you could be buying at wholesale or even getting free?)

44. Should the company Build It or Buy It? Own it, lease it, rent it?

45. **DIVERSIFICATION:** Why TUPPERWARE bought cosmetics/skin care product companies.

INTERNAL

TO DOUBLE(+) REVENUE, SAME # CUSTOMERS

STRAIGHT - LINES

PYRAMID

SPIDER - WEB

1.

PRICE STRATEGIES

$\rightarrow$

$\updownarrow$

2.

SELLING STRATEGIES

- Leading Up To Sale   +1%
- During/At Sale   +1%
- After Sale   +1%

               +3%

3.

LOSS PREVENTION STRATEGIES

With Leads	With Customers	In Operations
	Egs. Alarm Bells	

$+ 1\% \times 3 = +3\%$

$+ 3\% \times 3 = +9\%$

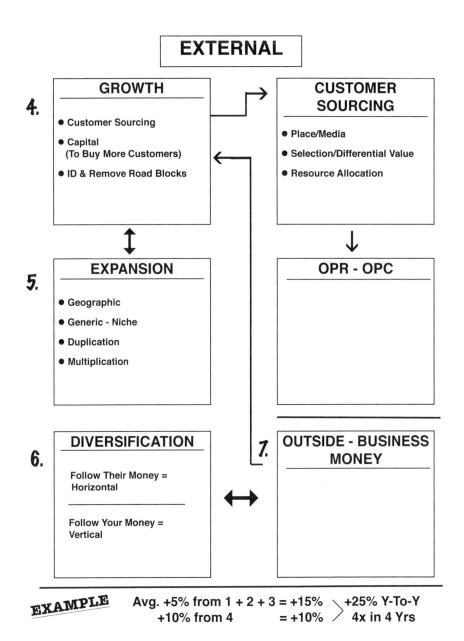

EXTERNAL

4.
GROWTH
- Customer Sourcing
- Capital
  (To Buy More Customers)
- ID & Remove Road Blocks

CUSTOMER SOURCING
- Place/Media
- Selection/Differential Value
- Resource Allocation

5.
EXPANSION
- Geographic
- Generic - Niche
- Duplication
- Multiplication

OPR - OPC

6.
DIVERSIFICATION
Follow Their Money =
Horizontal

Follow Your Money =
Vertical

7.
OUTSIDE - BUSINESS MONEY

EXAMPLE
Avg. +5% from 1 + 2 + 3 = +15%   +25% Y-To-Y
+10% from 4   = +10%   4x in 4 Yrs

MINI GLOSSARY OF TERMS

Appointment, No Sale. Refers to what happens after a potential buyer has gone through a sales presentation of some kind at a designated place and time and "escaped" without buying. In almost every instance, I prescribe complex, persistent, multi-step, multi-media follow-up ultimately including down-sells (lower priced or simpler or different offers).

Disaffection Alarm Bells. When do you want to know you have a "lost customer"? BEFORE he is lost. So, what "alarms" do you (a) have in place? … (b) monitor daily/closely? … (c) have a system ready to pull the trigger on, to stop the loss or rescue the lost quickly?

OPC: Other Peoples' Customers

OPM: Other Peoples' Money

OPR: Other Peoples' Resources

Subsidy: when another entity pays for part or all of your customer acquisition. Examples: sponsors an event or traveling road show; advertisers in your promotional magazine sent quarterly to accumulated unconverted leads; joint ventures and lead sharing; outright sale of lists or data. SECRET: almost every fast growth, small to big company has its growth subsidized.

FIND 3 WAYS TO ...

Increase size of <u>average</u> transaction

Increase size of <u>initial</u> transaction

Increase size of <u>top-of-pyramid</u> transaction

Increase <u>frequency</u> of transactions, <u>per customer</u>

Increase <u>frequency</u> of transactions, <u>top 20% of customers</u>

Increase <u>consistency</u> of transactions

Increase number of "<u>open doors</u>" (customer sources)

Increase *appreciated* <u>value</u> to customers

Improve <u>relationship</u> with customers

... REPEAT EVERY CALENDAR QUARTER

Acknowledgements to: Jay Abraham, Earl Nightingale.

DYNAMIC FINANCIAL EFFICIENCIES AND STRATEGIES,

In The Approximate Order
of First Appearance In This Book

1. **Advertising, marketing and growth-investment dollars can be de-valued before they even leave the nest! ... OR made worth more than their dollar valuation even before they are invested!!**

2. **Change your math, change your business, change your life.** *Every time* you change your math for the better, every other thing changes for the better. Find as many opportunities as possible to change your math. Look again next month. And again the month after that. And again and again and again.

3. **Money is *mobile*.** It moves by its own value system and self-interest, its own logic. Resistance is futile. It is incumbent on the business leader to envision Money's movements and align the business with them.

4. **Ask Money: *what do YOU think about this?*** Listen

very carefully to the answer.

5. There are many kinds of "theft" that commonly occur in the overwhelming majority of businesses. Lost dollars at the bottom line have to be replaced by generating 2, 3, 4 or more at the top. Therefore, **loss prevention can be extremely profitable.**

MAKING HIGHLY PROFITABLE DECISIONS ABOUT YOUR BUSINESS

6. **Only relevant and actionable information has potential value. Only APPLIED knowledge is power**. Discernment about what to know and what *not* to bother knowing is critical. There is far, far too much information, too many ideas, too many opinions to consume it randomly or by which purveyor yells the loudest or is most insistent. You have to have a process for managing the in-flow, for overt search and acquisition, and for being interested or disinterested in a source or an item.

7. **As much as possible, decision-making should be about:** *which works best – this or that? ...* from actual tests, not from opinions.

8. **Be *very* careful in your choice of Sales Culture or Marketing Culture for your business.**

INCREASING OR MULTIPLYING
THE VALUE OF EACH CUSTOMER

9. Anything less than a No-Fail Follow-Up System is leadership and ownership negligence. *Gross* negligence.

10. CUSTOMER VALUE needs creatively managed. If you present people with a spending ladder, many will climb it – having been pre-conditioned and trained to do so. If you present an ascension pyramid, the exclusivity of each higher level will motivate customers to ascend and will provide price and profit margin elasticity.

11. If you get a customer committed to "achieving" a goal that requires him to stay and spend (more; more frequently), you can dramatically improve that customer's total value to your business.

12. Find ways to be in front of your prospective customers, clients or patients ALONE, or at least ahead of everybody else. This can usually be accomplished by placing yourself where you are "*not* supposed to be".

BETTER PRICE STRATEGIES = BETTER
PROFITS

13. Under-pricing – usually in hope of buying greater

volume – is a common 'reverse alchemy.'

14. **Cost should be irrelevant in setting price**. Ignore normal and customary formulas, especially cost plus or cost multiplied by 'x.' Focus on the value to the customer and desire of the buyer, and what he can and will pay for that.

ERASING WASTE, INCREASING LEVERAGE

15. **Media Strategy is Place Strategy**. Do *not* go *anywhere* for the wrong reasons. Insist on it being profitable to be there. (If that sounds obvious, maybe it should be, but few business' media investing is *governed* by this one, simple principle.)

16. **Focus everybody and everything on one scoreboard: *sales***. (The legendary ad man David Ogilvy defined "great advertising" as: what sells. We can define "bad advertising" as what *doesn't* sell. And we can apply the same standard to every other activity or investment.)

17. **Democratized Spending is dumb. Be smarter.**

ABOUT THE AUTHOR
DAN S. KENNEDY

AUTHOR.

- Never off bookstore shelves since 1981.
- One of the most popular business book series: NO B.S.
- Over 1-Million Copies of all editions of all titles sold.
- Earned recognition on INC. 100 Best Books List, BusinessWeek Bestseller List, USA Today and more than 9-times on Amazon Bestseller Lists including #1.(Book List appears on Page 172)
- Created THE MAGNETIC MARKETING SYSTEM® - the #1 Bestselling Course on DIRECT Marketing For ANY Business.
- Created category-leading paid subscription newsletters with longevity of 25 Years.

CONSULTANT.

- Paid upwards from $19,000.00 a day/$3,000.00 an hour for strategy advice.
- Over 85% of all one-time clients repeat or continue.
- Many clients' tenure from 10 to 30 years.
- Many clients' businesses grown from start-up/small to $20-Million, $100-Million, even $1-Billion.

ADVERTISING COPYWRITER/
MARKETING MEDIA DEVELOPER.

- One of the highest compensation copywriters in the world.
- Typically engaged at 6-figure to 7-figure fees and royalties.
- Specialist in complete multi-step, multi-media systems.
- Holds records for longest running lead generation TV infomercial, project team participation on most valuable TV infomercial franchise, longest running online VSL (video sales letter). Portfolio includes over 100 direct response ads and sales letters each producing over $1-Million in revenue.
- Full-page print ads for clients in over 150 different publications.
- American Writers & Artists Copywriter of Year (2011).
- Over 85% of all one-time clients repeat or continue.
- Many clients' tenure from 10 to 30 years.

SPEAKER.

- 9 Years on the #1 Seminar Tour EVER In America: 25 – 30 Cities A Year, Audiences of 10,000 to 35,000.
- Career, over 3,000 compensated engagements.
- On own companies' events, appeared with many celebrity-entrepreneurs including Ivanka Trump, Kathy Ireland, Joan Rivers, George Foreman and Gene Simmons (KISS).

ENTREPRENEUR & INVESTOR.

- Founded and built the original publishing/membership company, now NO BS INNER CIRCLE.COM.
- Founding Investor in INFUSIONSOFT, the leading direct-marketing software for small to mid-sized businesses.

OTHER BOOKS BY THE AUTHOR

In the No B.S. series, published by Entrepreneur Press

No B.S. Price Strategy

No B.S. Brand-Building by Direct-Response

No B.S. Guide to Marketing to Boomers and Seniors

No B.S. Trust-Based Marketing

No B.S. Direct Marketing to NON-Direct Marketing Businesses

No B.S. Guide to Ruthless Management of People and Profits, 2nd Edition

No B.S. Grassroots Marketing for Local Businesses

No B.S. Business Success In The New Economy

No B.S. Sales Success In The New Economy

No B.S. Wealth Attraction In The New Economy

No B.S. Time Management for Entrepreneurs

No B.S. Guide to POWERFUL PRESENTATIONS, The Ultimate No-Holds Barred Plan To SELLING ANYTHING with Webinars, Online Media, Speeches and Seminars

Other Books by Dan Kennedy

SPEAK TO SELL (Advantage)

Ultimate Marketing Plan, 4th Edition – 20th Anniversary Edition (Adams Media)

Ultimate Sales Letter, 4th Edition – 20th Anniversary Edition (Adams Media)

Making Them Believe: 21 Lost Secrets of Dr. Brinkley-Style Marketing (GKIC/MJ)

Make 'Em Laugh & Take Their Money (GKIC/MJ)

Unfinished Business/Autobiographical Essays (Advantage)

The New Psycho-Cybernetics with Dr. Maxwell Maltz (Prentice-Hall)

FOREWORD BY
STEVE FORBES

A Must-Read for
ENTREPRENEURS,
CEOS, & LEADERS

AUTHORITY
MARKETING

How to Leverage 7 Pillars of Thought Leadership
to Make Competition Irrelevant

ADAM WITTY | RUSTY SHELTON

ForbesBooks

AUTHORITY MARKETING

ForbesBooks